Slices
Of Life

Published and distributed by Merack Publishing
Jackson, USA
www.merackpublishing.com

Library of Congress Control Number: 2025905686
Tedeschi, Joe
SLICES OF LIFE: AN ENTREPRENEUR'S LEGACY FOR MY
DAUGHTER

ISBN
Paperback 978-1-964421-07-0
eBook 978-1-964421-08-7

Slices Of Life

An Entrepreneur's Legacy
For My Daughter

Joe Tedeschi

Author Note

The stories I share in this book about the obstacles I have overcome, both personally and professionally, are from my memory and reflect its limitations. I've been fortunate to build businesses I am proud of, and I am grateful for the opportunities I have been able to create for my family—most importantly for my daughter Audrey, to whom this book is dedicated.

My Dearest Audrey,

Right now, you're seven years old—full of big ideas, and a smile that lights up my whole world. I'm writing this book for you so that one day, when you're ready, you can look back and understand my journey—the ups, the downs; the wins, the losses, and the moments I had to dig deep. I want you to see that no matter how big the challenge, you have the strength and courage to accomplish anything.

Yes, you'll read a lot about business, because that's been a big part of my life. But I want you to know that more than any deal, any company, or any success, the thing I am most proud of is being your dad. If I did everything else right but failed at that, it would all mean nothing. You are my greatest accomplishment, and the reason I want to leave something meaningful behind.

I Love You Always,

Dad

Contents

Introduction

The one thing that you have that nobody
else has is you. Your voice, your mind,
your story, your vision.
—*Author Neil Gaiman*

I was on the subway three times a week dragging a pizza cooler behind me, setting up an electric oven in a leading retailer's New York City offices at lunchtime.

"Do you like the crust? Do you *not* like it? Why? What can we improve?" I'd take feedback.

Then I'd go back and do it again. I'd get labels printed overnight, use hair dryers to blow dry cling wrap around the pies by hand, and do whatever else needed to be done to get our pizzas sold. Months later, we were rolling coolers of frozen pizza down the streets of the Bronx late at night, *Apprentice*-style, to get the product in a brand-new Duane Reade store by opening time. It was late fall, loud, bright, and a sweaty ninety degrees outside. We were late (thanks, Queens traffic), and I was anxious because we needed the cleaning staff to let us in by a certain time. By the time we got there, we weren't sure they could even hear us knocking on the windows!

It wasn't the most glamorous moment, yet within seven years, the company I'd joined to help out a college friend went from an 11,000-square-foot pizza crust manufacturing facility in El Segundo, California, to adding a 60,000-square-foot building—from fifty employees who had worked in a family business for decades to over 400 employees.

Seven years after that single Duane Reade opening in New York, we were the dominant player in the gluten-free pizza category, enjoying over 60% of the market space in North America. They called us the "Google boys of gluten-free pizza." The company grew from earnings of about a million dollars annually to become an enterprise with a nine-figure valuation!

We rolled our way up that hockey stick-shaped path and exited at the top.

I retired at fifty-five. It sounds like amazing luck. It sounds like a charmed path, like the ideal timing of *just* the right product at *just* the right moment, right? But that's not the story I'm telling you, because that's not the story we lived. My business partner Jimmy and I (with the support of my wife, Carla) fought all the odds. Others thought we would never make it, yet we launched a product in a relatively new category. And here we are, with a great—and all true—story to tell.

* * *

The story is good because it's textured. It's real, full of high highs and quite a few low lows as well. It was not *win, win, win.* It was more *win, loss, win, loss.* Like life.

My obstacles started at birth. I was born without the ability to see out of one of my eyes. After several years of trying to overcome and repair my disability, doctors determined fixing it was not possible without risky surgeries. I was told I may never drive, may never play sports. But while I was forced to accept my diagnosis, I could not accept the limitations. (I guess I've *never* taken no for an answer.) There had to be a way to fight through…to do what I knew I could do and find a way forward no matter what.

I proved this to be the case with a fairly successful sports career. In high school, I was a three-star athlete. I was also fortunate enough to work hard and become valedictorian of my graduating class, and that led me to get accepted into a few different universities, including my dream school, the University of Notre Dame. One problem: I knew it would be a challenge for my parents to afford private school tuition. Fortunately, I also applied to the University of Southern California, which offered me a full academic scholarship. At the time, I'd never been on a plane, or even out of New England!

As a freshman at USC, I tried out for the football team and was lucky enough to make the practice scout team as a walk-on, which I will admit was a remarkable feat. Football was everything to me, yet I was present for exactly zero kickoffs that year because I was outside the stadium selling T-shirts for spending money. I was happy to miss the beginning of every game because I had figured out what to do to get by. It was excellent training for all the businesses I'd go on to build after graduation.

Once I got cut from the scout team during my freshman year spring semester, I still wanted to keep playing. (Football may have been trying to tell me it was done with me, but I was not yet done with it.) I transferred back east to Central Connecticut State College, a Division III school, to keep playing. After one semester, I returned to USC and majored in Entrepreneurship, the perfect course of study as I'd always wanted to follow in the footsteps of my father, Joseph Tedeschi, Jr., who owned and operated his own contracting company.

I wrote a business plan around selling soft frozen lemonade in my senior year and ultimately ran or partnered in several businesses throughout my twenties and thirties. Just as I was gathering real steam, however, a stunning setback arrived, one I never could've anticipated nor planned for. I was diagnosed with a brain tumor, medically defined as a meningioma, and was out of work for a couple of years. (Remember what I wrote earlier about low lows? Yeah.) In a sense, I was ready to handle it due to the smaller challenges I had to overcome when I was younger.

In the aftermath of that life-altering experience, which you'll read more about in the chapters ahead, my good friend from USC, Jimmy DeSisto, offered me an opportunity to come out to California and help run his family pizza business, Venice Bakery.

* * *

Pizza has been around forever, and the conventional wisdom is that it's almost recession-proof. But when I joined, the industry was not changing. It was not factoring in the growing trend toward a more nutritional lifestyle. We were young and aggressive, so we were willing to innovate, to change things up. At the request of a holistic doctor, my partner Jimmy had developed our signature product, a vegan gluten-free pizza crust. As he began fielding more and more requests for it, he reached out to me to help grow the opportunity. I saw the potential and immediately said, "Let me see what I can do here on the East Coast."

Back in 2011, they thought we were crazy. Hardly anyone had ever *heard* of gluten-free pizza. But we believed in our product, and even though we didn't always know the correct next step, we were deeply invested in the business and grew it successfully. This book will tell you how we did it…mistakes and all.

My entrepreneurship story started early. From my soft frozen lemonade business to a coffee shop and lunchtime café I owned with my dad…from the mortgage company I ran with my brother to a software company that got raided by the feds (yes, really)…to the world of pizza, I learned what it takes to build businesses from the ground up successfully. I believe if you can succeed at building one business, you can take the foundational tools and experiences with you to have a very good chance of succeeding at building *any* business.

Before we jump in on all my wild ups and downs, however, I want to say two things about success. First, I view success as setting a goal and achieving it. Success is doing what you want to do and being happy with it. We often define people as successful based on their wealth—I may be guilty of this from time to time as well—but that's not a good measurement, because you can have unhappy people who have a lot of money, and conversely, you could have people who are very happy, who don't have that kind of money. We're all different; set your own goals. If you achieve them, you are successful *to you*. Maybe it won't matter to anybody else…that's fine. I want to be clear that when you read the word *success* in this book, you're considering it from the proper perspective.

Second, my successes in business have not been achieved solely due to my hard work. While hard work has had a significant impact on the outcome of my life, I do recognize the other required elements. I would be remiss if I didn't acknowledge that the support from my mother and father, associates and employees, and most importantly, my wife helped me get to where I am today.

Now that we've set the scene and given you a little preview of where we are headed, let's jump in by going back in time.

1

A Kid From Rhode Island

Growing up in the rural village of Hope in the small town of Scituate, Rhode Island, life was pretty simple. I was raised in a traditional middle-class family. Dad worked; Mom took care of the kids and everything at home. I'm the oldest of four. My brother Peter is one year younger than me, and my twin sisters Sandra and Susan are three years younger. We all went to the same local public school, Scituate Junior and Senior High School. While I shared a room with my brother, our sisters also shared one. There was usually a puppy and one or two cats in the mix, as well as a few pet birds and several fish. All three bedrooms were upstairs in our raised ranch, as were the kitchen, living room, and the one bathroom we all shared. We did have a shower downstairs, which really helped. Ha!

My brother was always a go-getter. Like me, he also loved sports, and he loved the social life. His gift of gab allowed him to be a very successful salesperson, whether working for others or himself. My sister Sandra was also very outgoing. She loved to be with friends and ride horses. Susan was the more athletic one. She loved to play softball, was a cheerleader, and loved her family. She is blessed today with a wonderful family herself, including her husband and two children currently attending the University of Rhode Island.

Mom was the rock! She held down the house and really made everything work. While Dad was the bread-winner, Mom made sure we all had our responsibilities met and the house was in order, all while always having dinner ready for the entire family! Dad was my mentor. A Korean War veteran, he taught me everything, like how to be a hard worker, a good husband, and a great father. I never saw him lose his cool; his temperament was steady beyond belief. But the most important thing he taught me was to be a good man. I owe everything to him and live my life knowing he would be extremely proud of me in so many ways.

As I look back at that time, I realize our house was a bit undersized for a family of six, but we didn't know any differently. I wasn't around people who had lots of money, and none of my friends' families had big homes. To us and everyone we knew, our lifestyle was typical of peers and of the middle class.

Every Tuesday and every Sunday, the six of us all had dinner together. Dad always made pasta and sauce, sometimes using tomatoes from our own garden. Family meals were a tradition we couldn't miss, not because we were forced to participate but because it was our routine…a delicious one. I remember Dad peeling and salting a cucumber he'd grown and handing it to me. There was nothing better than that first fresh bite! On Saturdays, Dad and I would visit my grandmother's house. I remember looking into the garden in the backyard and seeing her picking all the fresh vegetables she needed to make a salad. Sitting down at the table and talking to her and my aunts was a typical weekly visit that I counted on; we were close.

Our family all lived within a huge extended network of relatives. My father had three sisters. (My mother, unfortunately, lost her brother and her parents when we were young.) One of my dad's sisters also had four kids. My sisters are twins, and his sister had twins as well. Holidays were always big celebrations for us as an Italian family; the gatherings were *huge*. At my grandmother's house on Christmas Eve, for example, there were usually around twenty-five people, minimum. My father took this tradition over when my grandmother passed; then sadly, he passed away in 2018. Today, the tradition is carried on by my mother and continues with a nice large group. It's a chaotic but fun night, with lots of chatter and gift opening. But Dad and Mom loved hosting it because it was enjoyable and memorable each year. Sometimes the family gathering was so big that people would end up standing and grabbing a seat when someone did get up. We would bring the folding tables up from the basement and have to take them halfway out the front door and then around a corner just to get the tables up the stairs. Then, we would set the tables, trying to match each place setting, which never really matched. But in the end, who really cared? It was only family. These were, and still are, good times.

At Easter, Mom loved making her "lamb cakes." Shaped like a lamb, she would make dozens of them and deliver them to family and friends, where the cakes would then sometimes serve as a centerpiece for Easter Sunday.

Thanksgiving was another big event at my sister Sue's house. Mom would make her famous pumpkin roll, and she would often give out more of these to friends than her lamb cake at Easter. This holiday included more friends than family, and my brother-in-law would go to the live turkey farm and be sure to get the largest turkey available, regardless of the size that was needed. It was a treat, to say the least. Like many families, we all sat around after the feast and enjoyed our share of desserts while watching American football.

This close family bond was the foundation of my strength in my life.

Every summer, starting at an early age, we went to a local camp. There was a lot to do—all kinds of activities from learning how to swim to playgrounds to sports like baseball and basketball. We never traveled or went anywhere for vacation except for the Fourth of July when we took our annual three-hour car ride to Alton Bay, New Hampshire. There were ten to fifteen families in our group, and we all went to a place called Lake Winnipesaukee, where we rented cabins on the lake.

Our backyard abutted a farm with horses and cows. As you can imagine, it was fun. Trying to touch horses while they were sleeping was a favorite pastime with my friends. Thankfully, we had room in the side yard to play baseball. We would tear up the grass a bit to represent bases, which I'm sure didn't sit well with my mom and dad. There was also some room for us to add a basketball court, which my dad built for us, along with a little playhouse for the girls. It was a welcoming home for all our neighbors and friends, and I have lots of memories of after-school pickup games and kids being over. If he wasn't too tired, I often played catch with my dad after he got home from work. He bought me my first baseball glove and football and showed me, at an early age, how to throw and catch.

My father was able to take care of the family by owning and operating a contracting and construction business with a partner; they mainly built housing foundations. As his partner was nearing retirement, my dad started to branch out.

He said, "You know, maybe I can do more," and as a result began installing swimming pools. The first pool he installed was at our house in 1981. It took away space from our little side yard baseball field, but as we got older, having an inground pool was more fun for our age group.

* * *

I started playing sports when I was young, maybe seven or eight years old, and I always loved it. Dad was a big sports fan, which is probably what started me on my path to the fields and the courts.

Later, I played Pop Warner football (a nonprofit youth football league named for its founder Glenn Warner) and Catholic Youth Organization (CYO) basketball when I was about eleven years old. Besides Little League baseball, these were my first organized sports leagues. Because I had been playing two sports at home and at local parks, football was more challenging than the other games. It was my first introduction to a sport on a contact level, and I loved that type of teamwork.

During my Pop Warner days, I was often on the heavier and bigger size for the age group I played in. (Pop Warner levels and age groups also had weight restrictions.) Every Saturday night before Sunday game day, my dad would take me and another teammate of mine, Steve Alves, to the local YMCA. We would sit in the sauna for as long as we could—as long as we were allowed to without burning up—and sweat as much as we possibly could. And then, if we were still slightly above the weight limit, we would not eat for the rest of the evening. Usually, the games were in the late morning or right at noon. We did not eat until after the next morning's weigh-in. It was a difficult task, to say the least, but we were always able to make weight. My dad always had a couple of candy bars ready for us so we could get that initial rush of sugar to be ready to play in the game.

On one Sunday afternoon when I was about twelve years old, I was playing outside our home with my brothers, sisters, and friends when suddenly, I was in excruciating pain. My parents rushed me to the ER, where the doctors immediately determined it was appendicitis and that I had to go into emergency surgery before my appendix burst, which could have been toxic. That day was painful and frightening, and recovery lasted about a month.

In the first Pop Warner game after my surgery, I went back on the field and got the wind knocked out of me. I sat on the sidelines for a few minutes and then went back in to play and finished the game. Even at that young age, I couldn't turn off my desire to compete and win no matter what else was going on—or how I was feeling.

* * *

My speed on the field was an asset I leaned into in all the sports I played. It was recognized by others from the time I was young. On the baseball diamond, for instance, my speed made it easy for me to steal bases or beat out a ground ball to the infield for a hit.

I hit leadoff in the batting order thanks to my speed. I wasn't a power hitter. I wasn't the one who was going to go out and hit home runs or even doubles regularly, but to make contact and consistently get to first base on an infield hit was a positive characteristic to most coaches. Turning that single into a double was also something I could often do—or even a double into a triple. Speed absolutely contributed to my success in sports, and I enjoyed working on it.

As a freshman in high school, I was on the varsity baseball team. Even though I did not play often as a freshman, I traveled with the team to every game. Late in the game, if some other players were on base and it was close, I was the first substitute to replace them as a pinch runner to hopefully generate a run.

If I ever had a moment where I felt uncertain about an upcoming game, my dad always reminded me that my competitors on the field all put their pants on the same way: *one leg at a time.* His reminder gave me the courage to go out and compete confidently. When I had great games, Dad was right there to compliment me and support me. He also believed there was no need to tell everyone how good I was, as they could see it for themselves. His message naturally guided me to lead by example.

I carried these early lessons with me throughout life. It wasn't always easy, but I stayed true to what I knew was right and did my best so my teammates would do their best. There were times I had friends who did not want to be led by their friend; however, as a leader, I knew my responsibility, and my focus was on succeeding as a team since one person cannot be successful without the support of others. As a captain, I always reminded my teammates that we played for the name on the front of the jersey, not on the back.

My three sports all flowed continuously from one season to the next. I always played sports with older kids, which helped me develop my skills better. The challenge of playing with kids who were better than me was exhilarating. I was fortunate enough to work hard, do well, and eventually become captain of all three teams in high school.

* * *

When I was fifteen years old and a sophomore at Scituate High School, I was invited to a party of juniors and seniors, my teammates. I asked my parents if I could go.

I first asked my mother, who was upstairs, and she said, "Let's go ask your father."

My dad was downstairs watching TV. We went down to him, and I said, "There's this party I want to go to, but I need to know if it's okay with you if I go."

He sat there quietly, like always, and asked, "Is there going to be drinking?"

I was honest: "Probably."

He took his time, gave it some thought, and then nodded, saying, "You know the right decisions to make. Yes, you can go."

He trusted me to handle myself, which I did. That moment, when I look back on it, revealed that his trust in me was so valuable. I knew I could never let it go.

They say every man's story is a story about his father. I'm lucky I got such a good one.

2

Early Obstacles

A couple of things I had to overcome early in life helped me build self-confidence. The first was my eye—to this day, I am legally blind and can only see out of one eye. For years, I had to wear glasses with a patch. It was extremely humbling and embarrassing, and created a sense of insecurity because I stood out. My mother drove me to Boston to see doctors on a regular basis, trying to determine if there was any way I could get my vision back.

Unfortunately, this was not possible. It wasn't hard for me to adapt. It was just a part of my life. Since I was diagnosed at birth, all the deficiencies, handicaps, and self-conscious feelings related to my eye occurred when I was very young. Once I got to be about five years old, my parents informed me: nothing could be done, and the patch would not solve the problem.

Their finality was something I had to accept. At the time, it wasn't a conscious thing for me to say, "Oh, okay, I have to accept this and do the best I can." I was too young to have that clear reasoning ability. I simply did not know any differently and learned to live with the restrictions as a result of the deficiency.

I was exposed to German measles when I was pregnant with my son Joey. Ultimately, my exposure to this illness is where Joey's disability came from. It was a birth defect.

The day I came home from the hospital with him, he was lying on my lap in our apartment, and I noticed him looking up. One of his pupils was different from the other. When I saw this, I called the pediatrician right away. I had an aunt who was a nurse and had some connections with the Boston Children's Hospital. I drove Joey there regularly until we got some answers.

The only thing the doctors said could be done at that time would be an eye transplant. I said no. Once we realized there was really nothing more that could be done (though he was legally blind in that eye), my husband and I decided not to make a big thing out of it.

Joey excelled so much at everything, which made it easy to put our concerns about his eye aside. As the years went by, we saw him adapt and truly excel at sports each step of the way. My husband and I would sit

up in the stands and look at each other in amazement.
Joey adjusted so well; he didn't know any other way.

—Audrey Tedeschi, age 84 (edited for clarity)

My eye is still an issue as of today, but during my middle school and high school days, there was not any noticeable impact on me in terms of my physical looks. My vision was the same whether I had glasses on or off. When it came to sports, I had to alter my game a bit thanks to my eye, especially in baseball when I was batting by opening up my stance a little.

As time moved along in those early years, I didn't think my eye impacted me at all—although I revised that belief a little bit later when I was cut from the USC scout football team in the spring semester of my freshman year. You'll read more about this soon.

* * *

In addition to my non-functioning right eye, I also have a large birthmark on my stomach and was extremely self-conscious about it as a child. In the summers when we'd all go swimming, I kept my T-shirt on. The shirt provided a comfort level so I could at least get in the water.

When you're younger, things like this seem bigger than they really are. At the time, it felt like a "Why me?" situation.

But in the big picture, it wasn't a big deal. As you get older, your insecurities can sometimes find a way to become smaller. However, working through insecurities due to the physical differences I could not control was a process. I had to find a way to live with them and not worry about what others were saying or how they felt. It required me to start to look inside of me for what was true...not look to others.

Sometimes, I get emotional thinking about my younger days even now, fifty-plus years later, but I know when I started to look inside myself and realized *they don't mean anything*, I got stronger. My mom and dad gave me a big sense of security and competence because they made it seem as if my eye and my birthmark were no big deal. They were the first ones always to make me feel comfortable, to give me a strong foundation of self-worth.

* * *

When I was in seventh grade, I started attending a Catholic school not far from the house, but it did not click with me from the beginning. I cried daily. My parents found it best to take me out of the school, and I returned to my local Scituate Junior and Senior High School, where all my friends attended. I immediately became a much better student.

When I reflect on my younger days, one thing that stands out is how well-rounded I was as a student. In high school, for example, I tried to accomplish as much as I could.

I was vice president of the class. I was a three-sport star; I achieved All-Division honors in two of them; and I eventually became valedictorian of my class. Believe me, this is not something I was striving for; however, as I look back at it now, I think my desire *not* to fail was my driving force to achieve these accomplishments and this highly sought-after academic distinction, which I am proud of. I have always been extremely competitive, likely due to my early days of playing sports. This carried over to many facets of my life, and I consistently felt as if I had to do everything well, all the time. I trusted my gut with many decisions throughout life and made many decisions by instinct.

* * *

Though my parents didn't go to college, they stressed the importance of education to me and my siblings. I went to public school in town, but there was one major all-boys private high school, Bishop Hendricken, well-known for both academics and athletics. You had to take a test, similar to SAT and ACT exams, to get accepted. The general consensus was that if you wanted to play sports and eventually go to a big college, you *really* wanted to get into this school. Or, if you were excelling at academics and wanted to attend a big-name university, you also wanted in.

I was fortunate enough to get accepted there and even make the basketball team despite being a small fish in a big pond. Though these accomplishments meant a lot to me, and the conventional wisdom was that those who got into this school should stay there, I ultimately returned to Scituate High School. I felt I could be more of a leader as an athlete at my smaller school and shine academically as well—and I was correct about that. I listened to my inner voice and created my own path.

I can trace my inner ambition back to my dad, a man who always owned his business and served as a good example of a provider and survivor. (Born in 1932, he was drafted during the Korean War and honorably discharged after four years.) Dad came back from his time in the service and got to work, starting his own business and supporting his family…not just financially but emotionally. Dad was a calm, soft-spoken man.

My father was consistent with his message that it was okay to fail: "Do not be afraid to fall down or fail. You *cannot* get back up and succeed if you do not fall or fail," he said. Both he and my mom were crystal clear: their love would always be the same no matter what. No doubt thanks to his strong and steady influence, a feeling of always wanting to strive for better sits with me today. Is good enough acceptable to me? As long as I worked my hardest and gave it my all, yes. But knowing I can continue to improve at new things keeps me practicing them. Because from as far back as I can remember, I've known the only way I was going to keep up was to put in the time and practice. The only thing I could do—my only advantage—was my consistent willingness to work harder than everybody else.

3

Becoming A Trojan

Trust yourself. You know more than you think you do.
—Dr. Benjamin Spock

I attended the University of Southern California from September 1982 through May 1986. As a freshman, I originally thought I wanted to be an engineer and chose that as my major. However, after transferring back to USC for my sophomore year after a brief stint playing football for Central Connecticut, I decided being an engineer was not something I wanted to do...it was just a box I had checked at one point because it sounded good. To find my next move, I reflected on some wisdom from my dad: *owning your own business is where you will find true satisfaction and success from your own contributions.* (True, by the way.) Thus, I changed my major and graduated from USC's Entrepreneurship program, which has been consistently ranked as one of the top programs in the world.

When it came to making the decision to apply for USC, I didn't know much about the school, especially not about its academic excellence. As I was working with my guidance counselor, Mr. Anthony Ancona, in preparation for my high school valedictorian speech, I saw two unlikely applications sitting on his desk. One was for USC, and one was for UCLA. I had zero knowledge about the academic programs of either one. The only thing I knew was USC had a tremendous football program and a great rivalry with Notre Dame.

I said, "Let me try that one." I can't tell you what made me do it, but I did. I always think about what my life would have been like if I had gone to Notre Dame and had never even seen the USC application, but that's not what happened.

I was nervous to speak at my high school graduation; this would be my first public speaking opportunity. I'd also applied to the schools and colleges I really wanted to attend: Notre Dame; Central Connecticut because they had looked at me for football; a local school Providence College; and a school everybody said I couldn't get into, the University of Chicago (known for having a low acceptance rate, probably one of the lowest in the country; I knew it would be a challenge, so I accepted it full throttle).

As for actually giving the speech on the graduation ceremony day, I was *extremely* nervous—to the point of spiking a 102-degree fever and having to lie down and rest before it was time to go. Despite my nerves, I was able to push through and give it my best. (The fever cleared up before it was time to begin.)

In my speech, I talked with all my classmates about moving forward, all of us going in different directions. The majority of us had known each other from kindergarten all the way through twelfth grade. I spoke about how close we became as friends, the sports we played together, the activities we enjoyed, and how this was a time when, whether we were going to college five miles away or 3,000 miles away, or jumping into the workforce and getting jobs, any choice was going to be a new experience for everybody in the room.

I thanked our teachers and the school for all the opportunities presented to us, for allowing us to grow to be who we were becoming. I reflected on what we had accomplished together. The speech wasn't easy to deliver; I struggled a lot with conveying the right message amid my anxiety that day. I wanted it to be perfect. Speaking publicly has never been a strength of mine, but being able to do it when the occasion calls for it is part of growing up.

* * *

Since I had applied to USC, Dad and I went up to Boston to the local regional orientation for USC applicants in New England. We sat in a big room while recruiters from the university talked to us about the campus, including its pros and its cons. They gave us a true insight into what to expect and how to handle ourselves. Then, I went in for a one-on-one with the recruiters and outlined why I wanted to go there, what my credentials were, and gave the outline of my accomplishments in high school. I remember being polite, respectful, and very sincere. It was a full eight-hour day. When I got back, I had no idea what the result would be.

A few days later, I received the acceptance letter from Notre Dame. It was a dream come true; I did not believe I would go anywhere else. However, when I sat down with my parents, I realized we couldn't afford $8,000 a year. It was well beyond my family's means. They asked me if this was really what I wanted to do, to be the first of our family to go to a college far away. It was important to me, and they supported me and said they would take out a second mortgage to afford the steep tuition.

I submitted my letter of intent to Notre Dame with $500 the next day. Approximately 48 hours later, however, I received notice I was getting a full academic scholarship to USC. You could say that I was mature enough at that age to realize this was a no-brainer. I knew I could not put my parents in the position of having a second mortgage if there were another option. And I'd just found out there was.

It was an easy decision. But it was also, truly, a random kind of process that got me out to California. There was just something inside of me saying, "You've got to try," and it changed the rest of my life. (It's weird how these life choices, even the subconscious ones, lead you to where you want to be. If you trust your gut and expand your horizons and believe that, *you know what, I could probably do this. I might be scared, but I'm strong enough to do this*, you'll mostly be alright.)

Before I started college, the only time I'd been out of the state of Rhode Island was for our annual summer vacations to New Hampshire. That was it. Getting on a plane for the first time, then, was a scary—very, *very* scary—adventure.

When I landed and got settled, I was extremely homesick. I called home the next morning crying.

* * *

As I think about my childhood and my high school and college days, one thing my mother and father never did for me was solve my problems. They were there to support me at *all* times but left it up to me to sort things out. This lesson is so important in a child's development that it cannot be stressed enough. As much as we try to help our children and do not want them to struggle, one of the most important gifts we can give is the ability to allow our children to figure things out for themselves. College was when I gained a lot of my self-esteem and self-confidence. Navigating it led me to start feeling proud of myself and become more confident that *I* had the ability to solve the problems and issues that came my way.

A good example of this policy of theirs unfolded right here in my story: when I called home within twenty-four hours of landing in Los Angeles. I begged my mother to let me come back home. She convinced me the best thing for me was to stay and wait until they came out for parents' weekend to evaluate the situation.

My mother said, "You know, in thirty days we'll be there. It'll be Parents Weekend before you know it. Let's just wait it out. And if we come out there and you still don't like it, we'll figure out something to do."

This was one of the greatest gifts she gave me, and I bet it was not easy for her.

So they did exactly what she promised; they came out. I got through those first thirty days, trying to meet people and finding friends I thought I would blend well with.

Two days after I arrived, before I'd had the chance to meet everyone on my dorm floor, I received a care package my mother had sent overnight. My dorm mate from next door brought over a box and asked, "Is there anybody by the name of Joe Tedeschi here?"

I said, "Yeah, that's me."

"I think this is for you. They brought it to my room. My name is Joe Tedesco."

It was like, *wow*…was it a small sign I was on the correct path? I'm not sure, but it did feel like it. I'm still good friends with Joe today. It was those types of little things that made me feel comfortable: getting to know the school, getting to know the campus, meeting new people. Thirty days later, I was much more comfortable with the situation and the environment…and I knew California was probably the right place for me.

* * *

It was difficult at first, but I needed that push to learn who I was. The experience of moving so far away for school taught me to grow up, to understand responsibility, to see what it meant to take care of myself—to make my bed and do my laundry like any kid would have to do.

The biggest thing I learned in those years was how to be on my own, take care of my responsibilities, and find myself. I didn't have any family in California and no one to turn to who was physically close to me. We did not have the technology options for communication we have today, so this was a critical point in my life when it all became real. That was the time for me—when I knew I had to become an independent and confident man. It was a quick realization, but it helped me become who I am today.

There were many things I was not used to as an eighteen-year-old kid on my own in another state, not really knowing anyone except for the few friends I had just met. It taught me to go out there and figure it out! No excuses. No one was going to do it for me. This is a lesson all young adults must learn...and will learn at some point in their lives.

The different culture in California was a total shock. Since I was from a you-did-what-you-had-to-do kind of place, the wealth I saw was something *else*. Although my dad owned a successful business to support our family, we were not from an opulent environment. The definition of wealth where I came from was completely different from where I lived now. Where I came from, if you had a million dollars, everybody felt you were rich and treated you as such (sometimes, not for the better). While I always thought of my future self in those days as a person who would strive to be wealthy and successful, it was never to a California level because I didn't even *understand* the California level when I was eighteen.

Nevertheless, my earliest goals for myself were pretty ambitious...and surprisingly accurate. When I was about twenty-two years old, I remember thinking to myself, "I'm going to retire at fifty-five." And that's exactly what I did. I didn't know how or where I would be when I got there; I just knew reaching my goal would not be easy, and I would have to work hard to achieve this ambition.

In any case, USC presented a totally different environment and culture than what I was used to back in Rhode Island. To be specific, I was seeing eighteen-year-old kids getting brand-new cars. My first car was a $300 Plymouth Valiant. (It was a relic even then.) I graduated to a 1971 Pontiac Firebird when I was eighteen. I thought it was cool, but then I saw kids with brand-new Corvettes!

It was a complete surprise to me. Some of the friends I met and bonded with were in a situation where they would have their brand-new sports cars from home sent to them on trailers. Although they obviously came from wealthy backgrounds, they were down-to-earth individuals and friends once I got to know them. I saw a new level of wealth and started to feel it was achievable. It was no longer "out there," but familiar.

If I had not met a group of friends who hadn't also shared in some of these luxuries, I might have thought, "Okay, this is too much for little ole' me. I'll never be there." But part of it made sense to me after I got to know the person behind some of these luxuries. It became real.

4

College Football & Graduation

When I made the choice to attend USC, I did not think I would ever play football again because I wasn't highly recruited out of high school, especially not at Division I schools. Still, I had the same mindset about sports that I had when I applied to get into the school itself: *Why* not *try out for the team? What's the worst-case scenario? If you don't make it, you're in the same position you're in now.*

I went into the athletic department at the beginning of the season and asked if there was an opportunity to try out. I was a small, five-foot-eight-inch, 178-pound kid who had no right being on that football field among guys with athletic scholarships for my position who were much bigger than me and highly recruited. I bulked up to 184 but couldn't do anything about my height, obviously. Still, they let me try out and put me through the paces. I was not the biggest kid or the strongest kid, but as I described in the first chapter, I was an extremely *fast* kid.

When I was clocked in at under 4.6 seconds for the 40-yard dash that tryout day, some eyes opened up. My speed is what got me accepted on the scout team. It was very competitive out there. Others were doing these speeds as well, so at least I had the ability to fit in with those kids who were there on scholarships, and it got me the opportunity to play again. One of the USC coaches, Ted Tollner, and a defensive player, Riki Gray, called me into the office and asked, "Why do you want to do this? Do you know how hard this is? You know you're undersized and you could get hurt?"

"I get it," I said. "It's just something I love to do, and I am not ready to give up."

"Okay," they nodded. "We just want to lay this out to you."

Even though they made it clear I was very undersized, they still offered me the opportunity to play. I wasn't deterred by the warning, because I had always played with older kids. I may have been younger and smaller, but I knew that by working harder than anyone else, I was going to keep up. Each night during my freshman year, I drove to the beach with my friends who were very supportive and ran in the sand to get faster and stronger. This was my competitive advantage, and I loved enhancing the talent that I had.

I overheard some rumblings, mainly, "He's too small," but I proved myself. The work I did up front in the weight room to put myself there, and the persistence of going into the athletic department and asking for a tryout, for a kid who had no right being on that field, was undeniable. Just *being* there was a big achievement…especially when you compared me to my teammates. This was a Division I top-notch football program.

Immediately upon making the scout team, the coaches advised me to go see an academic guidance counselor. The counselor was the one who helped pick the classes and the teachers specifically for student-athletes…to make it possible to both attend classes *and* be there every day for practice as well as time in the weight room. Because I initially thought I would be an engineer, I picked classes according to the requirements of that program, which were very difficult and spread out through the day. With the workload that was required for the football team, however, I couldn't take classes in the afternoon. I had to be in the trainer's room, then I had to be on the field. As a result, the guidance counselors had to help me choose classes to fit that schedule.

I got creative about earning money in my first year in college. Between campus and the student apartments, everybody knew about this one guy who was a non-student and a popular off-campus vendor. He used to sell the newspaper and different magazines, as well as a small selection of USC T-shirts. From watching him, I then had an idea for a little side hustle.

I thought, *What if I expand on this idea a little bit and sell T-shirts to students for the games outside and closer to the stadium?* Since I was on the scout team, I had to be there for every practice, but I didn't have to suit up for the games.

There was an opportunity because the USC bookstore and this vendor were selling basic T-shirts for USC, and I had some ideas for designs they weren't offering. I picked his brain, asking, "Where do you get these printed?" and he gave me a couple of leads. I came up with some more relevant Game Day T-shirts based on who the team was playing for each home game and got them printed. (For instance, the most popular shirt in my roster had a common rivalry UCLA insult on the front, haha.) My shirts resonated with the students more than a basic USC campus T-shirt.

It was not some extravagant venture; I was not reinventing the wheel. It was more like, *I see something interesting here. Let's see if I can maybe make it better.* Actually, many great businesses are started with a thought like this one.

I laid the shirts out on the sidewalk so people could see them as they streamed into the stadium. When I saw a cop or a security guard, I'd pack everything up quickly and move along. I was selling maybe fifty shirts per game at $10 a pop, a good week's pay for an eighteen-year-old kid.

* * *

After my one-and-only season on the team, I got cut in the spring for the next year but still felt I could play. Therefore, I called my high school coach and asked, "Can we get in touch with Central Connecticut?" This was one of the schools looking at me in high school, so I wanted to go out and see if there was still an opportunity to play there.

Fortunately, the coaches did invite me to visit. After watching some film, the team ultimately said, "Yes, we feel you could play here—but you should know, there's no scholarship available."

I did some research and went to the administration office at USC to talk to them about transferring temporarily. I didn't want to transfer for the rest of my college career. I wanted to graduate from USC, so I made my intent to return clear to them. I found out I could take up to twelve credits elsewhere and not lose my academic scholarship eligibility—and that I could return to USC without reapplying. So, I went back east and transferred to Central Connecticut for the fall semester of my sophomore year. I wasn't ready to be done with football—that was the main reason for this move. Also, the fact that I was able to go back home on weekends and my family was able to come out to games to watch me play was very satisfying. However, I did not feel Central Connecticut could afford me the opportunities that USC could, particularly given the USC academic scholarship still waiting for me. (I took out student loans to help pay for my tuition for that single fall semester in Connecticut, however.)

Playing in the snow and dealing with inclement weather was harder than I remembered it being in high school as well. "What am I doing?" I said to myself. "This is crazy." I thought, *You know, my fingers are freezing. My toes are freezing. I just came from eighty-degree weather to suffer through this? I don't like it.*

I returned to USC in January of my sophomore year and met another student named Jimmy DeSisto in the dorms—Parkside Tower, to be exact. We became friends and played a lot of intramural sports together, mainly flag football. This relationship would become lifelong.

1980s Technology

I was introduced to a new technological device during my senior year in college called a computer. Seems odd now to reflect on a computer as "new." As a student majoring in entrepreneurship, I wasn't sure what all the benefits of having a computer would be (although it was obvious relatively soon). I just knew it would help me not only in school but also in any business I wanted to pursue. I called my parents for the money to buy one. They were initially reluctant…since they did not know what a computer was or what the benefits would be.

After explaining it to them, they found a way to send me the money, being as supportive as they always were. Computers back then were bulky and sat on a desk like a big box, similar to the old televisions that the previous generation was used to. I had to take computer classes to understand how they worked, but I quickly saw the benefits. Learning to program this new machine did seem overwhelming and challenging…we were working in DOS, a very early computer language! But the end result was so satisfying. There was something about computers, and cutting-edge tech in general, that I've always loved. As we all know, they've come a long way and are now second nature to business and everyday life.

I don't think there was a time when my parents didn't support my decisions. Though using the computer wasn't required in school, it was such a hyped-up resource, a tool I thought I would need in the future. Initially, it really helped when it was time to write a business plan during my senior year for my program. Long term, it helped that my enthusiastic adoption of technology started early in life.

* * *

We had a lot of college-kid fun…some innocent, some not-so-innocent. My roommates and I used to drive to Vegas, four hours away. We'd spend $20 sitting at the fifty-cent poker table, which would last us for hours, then drive back, sleep, get up the next morning, and do it again! Crazy: yes. Innocent: yes. Worth it: probably not.

One time when I was a senior, Joe Tedesco and I had a plan to get some lunch on a Sunday. We were walking toward the elevator in our apartment. Someone was coming out at the same time and said, "Hey, you guys want tickets to the LA Rams game?"

"Sure, why not?" we responded.

We grabbed the tickets, and instead of going to lunch, we drove over to where they were playing not far away in Anaheim. We really didn't want to go to the game, we just wanted to sell the tickets to make money. Once we got there, we had people come up to us to ask how much and we said $20—face value was $18.

Two people approached us, and once the money was exchanged, they identified themselves as undercover cops. We were like, *uh-oh*. Because we were selling above face value, it was considered scalping. (Now you can go on Stub-Hub and pay multiples of the face value and it's okay, but things were different then.)

They took us into the security office of the Rams stadium and said, "Okay, we need your identification." Joe was driving, so he had his ID. I wasn't driving, so I didn't have identification. They let Joe go and took me into a holding cell inside the stadium. I got to make one phone call. I made my call to my roommate, James Chae. He thought I was kidding and hung up the phone, so they kept me there.

I was sitting there by myself wondering, *How am I going to get out of here?*

The only thing I could hear in there was the radio coming through on the intercom. It was the Rams game. Great. Not exactly what I wanted to listen to right then!

A couple of hours later, Joe and our fourth roommate came down and bailed me out. Months later, I had to go back to the court and go through the process. Fortunately, the judge dismissed the charges. Crazy: yes. Innocent: not so much. Worth it: definitely not! Haha.

As I think back on my past, I see that no matter how much fun and trouble I got into as a young adult, I always had certain internal guardrails in place that helped me keep one foot on the ground and never step too far out of bounds in terms of the choices I made or the risks I took. The first of these guardrails was my father's love and trust in me to do the right thing. The second of these was my own self-concept, the part of my personality that liked to accomplish things and achieve good results. These two factors kept me moving forward in life to positive places, and I am grateful for them.

Graduation

Since I was the first in my family to attend and graduate from college, everyone was excited for me. I was able to do everything I wanted to do in school (even leaving for a semester to play football) by being resilient, determined, and motivated from start to finish. This meant I was able to graduate in four years. I thought graduating that fast was such an accomplishment...I wanted to reach the goal of finishing school sooner rather than later. I was a young kid who came from a family that really didn't have any college experience. Although my family did not have any college education, I did know the conventional wisdom: if you were fortunate enough to afford it, you went to college for four years, graduated, and got a job. When I think about it now, I wish I had taken my time! I may advise my daughter to take the five-year program because there's so much time left in life that you will have to work, so I want her to enjoy that college experience.

During my college years, I went back home every summer. The first year, I returned for every holiday as well. Over time, those visits decreased because of the new friends I was making and the new families I was being introduced to and being welcomed in. For example, after meeting Jimmy my sophomore year, I went with him to some holiday celebrations at his family's house, and over time, I came to think of his mom, Anita, as my West Coast mother.

When I graduated, my whole family came out to attend the ceremony. It meant a lot to me, and the entire week was a purely fun time. During the day, many activities were going on at my school. At night, we stayed in the hotel, laughed, and had dinner together...moments that I will cherish forever. It was also nice for Jimmy and his family to get the chance to meet all my siblings, as his mom had completely taken me in. Anita has a nice relationship with my mother to this day. When I graduated, I actually moved in with her and stayed for about six months before finding my own apartment in Fullerton.

I want to highlight this moment when my entire family came out to California simply to celebrate me and my accomplishments, and thank everyone. When it comes to the closeness a family can have as the children are growing up, even if the dynamic changes later on as we get older, it doesn't mean the memories of being together stop being important. Those memories endure and live inside of us forever.

5

Soft Frozen Lemonade

My dad's day began when he'd get up at 6:00 a.m. every day. He even put in a shift bartending at the local Italian-American club every Saturday as all members did, yet he and Mom somehow always made time to be at all of the kids' sporting events. In fact, Dad often came home from a long day's work and took us to or picked us up from one of our practices while Mom stayed home to make dinner and take care of the house. I watched him go downstairs to his office every night before dinner to summarize the day and get ready for the next day.

My parents instilled strong values in me. Their way of life—their deep integrity—was the only thing I knew. It was the norm for me. Hard work is truly a trait that has made me successful.

When I was in high school, at the age of fifteen, I worked at a gas station after school. It was my first job. During the summer, after working at the gas station, I parked cars at a summer concert venue across the street. I was motivated to earn as much money as I could. Later on, although I attended college on a full scholarship, I still needed spending money. In between my classes, I worked for the university's travel agency to deliver tickets to the faculty.

Each summer, I returned home and got a job working with my dad. Every morning, we drove to each of his employees' homes to pick them up. Almost all of his employees did not have their own cars. Therefore, he sat outside their homes each morning, beeped the horn, and waited for them to come out. Next, he drove to the coffee shop, where he would buy everyone coffee and donuts while he did his paperwork to get ready for the day's job. Not only did he start the day like this, but he also bought his people lunch and then took them home each day!

It taught me a great deal about being a business owner and having the responsibility of taking care of others, even on days when they were not ready to do so themselves. I never once saw him frustrated about picking everyone up each day. It was what he knew he had to do. What it taught me was how we have to care for our employees and make sure they are happy and enjoying their work.

That act of kindness and generosity on my dad's part was returned to him by his employees' gratitude and loyalty. They looked forward to working for him—*not* his competitors.

West Coast Lemonade

Seniors in my major at USC had a whole year to write up a business plan. While the Entrepreneurship program was young and relatively new back then, I knew instinctively that what they were asking us to do was a great opportunity disguised as an assignment. When I saw my friends writing their business plans just to get by and graduate, I thought a more appropriate way to do it—since I knew I wanted to learn how to run a business—was to actually start a business and write the plan as I was growing it in the real world.

We were well prepared to complete this assignment. Our professors, including Mr. Thomas O'Malia, helped us understand all the components. I loved the Entrepreneurship program because it offered us a taste of everything…we got to study a bit of marketing, a bit of advertising, a bit of finance, as well as some management. It was a well-rounded program, which was important to me as I did not want to have the tunnel vision most other majors can experience.

I wanted a little bit of the knowledge of *everything*—a "jack of all trades, master of my domain" mindset. Realizing that it was up to me to put all the pieces together as a foundation for a business moving forward, I quickly learned that when you're actually starting a small business, you need to see the whole picture. You can't always hire help right away; you have to figure things out using what you've learned or what you have the sense to research. Therefore, my "little bit of everything" program helped me in the real world.

The first problem, of course, is always the same: Am I meeting a need? If so, then I need to get people to know about me and what I'm selling. Then, the next question is, "How do I offer this product or this service at a reasonable cost? A cost that is perceived as a great value to those that it is intended for."

* * *

In 1985, while still in school, I started a soft frozen lemonade business, a product that was extremely popular on the East Coast, especially where I came from. I couldn't find anything like it on the West Coast at that time. To get started, I bought an old post office truck. I took it to Maaco, where I was able to paint it green and yellow for $99. I added a big yellow lemon and bright yellow words of my company West Coast Lemonade (creative, I know).

Starting this particular kind of business happened almost by default because our family had a relationship with one of the two biggest soft frozen lemonade businesses in Rhode Island. My dad reached out to the owner of one, and he helped us source the equipment needed. He was very unselfish regarding sharing the fresh lemon, sugar, and water formula. (Although simple ingredients, the secret was really the precise *ratio* of these ingredients, and the mixing machine needed to obtain the proper consistency.)

I bought twenty-pound bags of sugar and had a water line connected to the machine. After manually squeezing lemons each morning equal to what was needed for a five-gallon container, I added the correct amounts of water and sugar to the mix. I put a small chest freezer in the truck, which held up to six five-gallon containers and lasted me approximately six hours on a medium-busy sales day.

Driving around the neighborhood close to where I was living in Fullerton, California, I wanted to get people familiar with my route. They'd know I was reliable: "Okay, at three o'clock in the afternoon, the lemonade truck, just like the ice cream truck, will be here." I gave my product away for free for about a month to introduce it to people in hopes of them loving it. I could see there was an interest in the product, so my next thought, after I started charging for it, was, *How do I expand this?*

I could have purchased another truck and gone to another area, but I didn't feel this was the most efficient move at that time, for liability reasons. Still, things were going well. After I graduated, I continued to think about ways to build my business. There was only so much product that could fit in the truck, so I bought a lemonade cart and painted it just like the lemonade truck. I hired a young employee to help out by selling refreshments at local swap meets and flea markets on the weekends. Therefore, I was solving a need. I then worked on getting known regarding the product I was selling. My costs were determined, and I was able to put a price on each cup that was fair to all while allowing for a profit.

This led to my first interaction with Jimmy on a business level. I wanted to find another source of revenue while my new employee was sitting in one spot for six hours. Therefore, I decided to set up a pizza stand behind the lemonade cart. We had a 10' x 10' area, and we found there was a lot of dead space behind us. We hooked up a little pizza oven and hired a second person. This allowed me to maximize the revenue from the stall I was already paying for. Jimmy was working in his family pizza business that year, so all my pizza supplies came from him on generous terms.

I was selling slices of pizza and cups of lemonade from the same spot. Figuring out what I needed to sell the slices of pizza for was relatively straightforward. The "rent" was already fixed; and I knew my cost of goods (crusts, sauce, toppings, etc.). Revenues immediately increased.

* * *

Maintaining the books was not difficult. Payroll was easy since we had only one or two employees at first, and payroll taxes were straightforward to manage. Typical of many entrepreneurs starting their business, I began with just me as the only employee.

Handling the admin tasks in addition to running the day-to-day operations required long hours. I remembered how my dad handled the long hours and did whatever was needed, so this did not deter me. (I know the admin tasks associated with starting your own business may seem overwhelming, but with the right mindset and desire to succeed, these tasks can be easily achieved. They will organically fall into place through trial and error, or you'll figure it out by asking other entrepreneurs for advice.)

I used my computer to track revenue with simple spreadsheets. When I started out, I was working seven days a week. Monday through Sunday, I wrote down how much money we collected. I didn't have a business credit card; I was writing a regular paper check for my ingredients and balanced my account manually in the ledger. It was straightforward: For example, QuickBooks was extremely beneficial for me. It was the simplest and most useful tool I had. Thanks to QuickBooks, it was easy to submit a Financial Statement at the end of the year to my accountant. This process was somewhat familiar to me because of school. Unfortunately, there were no big write-offs for me to take advantage of.

My Entrepreneurship program at USC was directly relevant to being in business with the soft frozen lemonade company. It helped me figure out answers to questions like, "Does this business make sense financially?" (finance); "What do I do next?" (execution); "How do I get known?" (marketing). It made me think about creative ways to get the new or existing customer to understand why my product was worth it. My marketing for the lemonade was all about location, meaning I went to populated areas, to businesses such as car dealerships and local neighborhoods. Since the salespeople sat around and looked at every single vehicle that came in, they had a lot of time to come out to my truck for three minutes to get lemonade. Selling from flea markets was also good marketing because there was a lot of foot traffic in a small area.

Next, I started knocking on doors with the goal of getting my product into a local theme park. Six Flags Magic Mountain was doing a pilot program with another soft frozen lemonade company from Florida. It was the first time the product was distributed in Southern California; Disney didn't even have it yet. I went up to Magic Mountain and did the whole dog and pony show for them. I said, "Hey, listen, if anything happens with your pilot program supplier, I'm here. Give me a call."

And they did!

After the season, which ended after Labor Day, I got the call.

They said, "We're looking for another vendor."

I did my presentation for them again, and we agreed to a split of revenue. They explained to me that this was the type of business structure they had in place with the previous supplier, and that they wanted to have the same arrangement with me. We also worked out some business terms I would have to adhere to. Not only did they want an even split of revenue, but it was up to me to incur the cost of build-out of the locations throughout the park where I would be selling lemonade. It felt like a huge deal to me (and it was), so I called my dad and said, "I'm in over my head here and may need your help."

I explained all of the details, and of course, he was as supportive as ever. Dad came out the first week of October to help me.

Two days later, a crushing blow. I got a call saying, "Hey, we renegotiated with our previous vendor, so we're going to stick with him." To this date, I am not sure exactly what happened, but I believe new terms were negotiated that were unknown to me.

It was a harsh wake-up call. I was stunned.

My dad and I talked about it. He said, "Sometimes this happens in business."

"You know, it's helping me understand the ups and downs of business," I replied, shaking my head. I was a twenty-two-year-old kid, and I didn't know how these decisions were made. I just thought I had a good product. They called me! They loved it, right? Done deal. But there was so much more to it than that.

There were other factors that contributed to closing a deal in this situation, and I didn't know what they were back then, but I quickly learned. Maybe I should have done more, been on top of the decision-makers more closely at Magic Mountain. They already had a personal relationship with the other vendor, while I had an incomplete understanding of their needs because I didn't have that relationship. He was a proven entity and a better negotiator while I was just a number—and I was number two.

Upon reflection today, I see that when I did experience business success later on, it was because I was deeply engaged with the customer. I had more than a business relationship with buyers in many situations; these were personal relationships built on trust. The type of understanding and bonding that happens over months, or even years, is everything.

But back then, I felt deflated. I wanted to return to familiar ground. It felt then as if I didn't know anybody very well in California. I didn't have those deep personal relationships (or, it felt like I didn't have enough of them). So, I ended up selling everything—my truck, my equipment, and my formula—to another vendor who had been operating at the same events I had served and decided to go home to Rhode Island.

However, despite my challenges with this early enterprise, I'd tell any young person who wants to start a business,

"Don't wait. As FDR famously said, the only thing to fear is fear itself." You can do it while you're in school, which is what I did, or you can even delay school if that is where your path leads you. If you continue to wait until you think you are ready, you'll be waiting for the rest of your life. If it doesn't work out because you have no idea what you're doing, you'll have plenty of time to figure it out and try again, or do something else. The best way to learn how to run a business is actually to run a business.

6

Coffee Caffe

When I came back to Rhode Island, I took about six months off to get over the disappointing situation with Magic Mountain. I felt kind of down. But then reality set in: *I have to go back to work.* A job with GMAC, the financing division for all General Motors products, was one of the first opportunities that came along. I jumped on it, wanting security, a reliable paycheck at the end of the week, and the match in my 401k. After a year, I saw the account building, and it felt good.

They put me in what was known as the SEIT program, which stood for *salary employee in training.* It was an accelerated supervisory program whereby you spent six months in four different departments to train to become a supervisor in two years. While I was in the finance department, I was the one looking at the paperwork to make the decision on car buyers' financing approval, for example.

It quickly became routine and boring. I thought GMAC would be the safe route—and it probably would have been, but I definitely would not have achieved the happiness and success that I've reached had I stayed. Nevertheless, working there was a worthwhile experience because it taught me to recognize what I did *not* want to do. After two years, I looked around and thought, *I don't want to be where these corporate people are in twenty or thirty years.*

However, I did meet some intelligent individuals during my time with the company, and I remember specifically being intrigued by an idea one of my GMAC peers mentioned. He said, "Why don't we sell computers online?"

It was obviously a good idea; this was not long after Dell's online computer business model was taking off. Selling computers online was interesting to me even though I didn't know anything about it. It just tickled the entrepreneurial part of my brain, something I couldn't deny was a huge part of who I was…and wanted to be.

* * *

Before I write about my next venture, I want to pause and describe a serious health episode of my sister that affected me and everyone in our family. At the age of twenty-one, Sandra began getting typical lupus symptoms. There were rashes and some pain in her joints. We had no clue at the time what was going on; I'd never even heard of Lupus. She went to the doctor, and after a few visits, they talked to us about this disease. It continued to get worse instead of better.

Sandra had to go into the hospital for additional tests, and while we were all standing around the bed, she had a stroke in front of us. It was tough to witness. We had no idea what was happening; we were calling the nurses and panicking. She had become suddenly unresponsive, just staring out and not moving. She was not talking to us, not looking at us, even though we were repeatedly calling her name.

"Sandra! Sandra! *Sandra!*"

She couldn't respond. The nurses told us what was happening, and we had to clear the room, which was scary. The cause of the stroke was uncertain because it could have happened for many reasons.

My father was a quiet man. He took everything in before he'd react or respond. Dad really didn't say much about Sandra's situation or the reasons for it. But my brother and I were somewhat different. I was always extremely protective of my sisters as the oldest boy in the family. It was just a role that, as an Italian man, would pass down to me—being the protector of the family. I wished there was more I could do for her, then and now.

There was a lot of rehab needed after a stroke like the one my sister had. My dad would not go to work and sit there in the hospital with her every single day. After her discharge, she went to a rehab center in Braintree, Massachusetts. She had to stay for a period of time, so he stayed there with her every day as well. At this time, I was in the collections department at GMAC and on the road all day, every day. During that part of the program, I had a flexible schedule and went to visit Sandra almost every day as well…just to be with her, like Dad was.

After her time in Braintree was over, Sandra had to continue outpatient rehab at home, and that transition is where she lost all of her motivation.

However, Sandra still wanted to go back to how she was living prior to her lupus diagnosis and stroke, so she went out with her friends on occasion and fortuitously met the man who is now her husband. He unequivocally 100% loves her the way she is, and they do not want for much. They don't ask anybody for anything. Truly admirable, to say the least.

* * *

After about two years, I knew GMAC wasn't for me. I was not comfortable with a nine-to-five job and the structure that came with it. I left my job and returned to the world of entrepreneurship—where you'll work harder and longer than you ever would at any regular job.

After thinking about what I wanted to do next, I heard about an opportunity to purchase a failing café in the capital city of Rhode Island. My dad and I went to check it out and figure out if there were any obvious signs as to why it was failing and why it may be for sale.

Coffee Caffe was located on South Main Street in Providence, an area that was near Brown University and the state courthouse. There was a well-established deli next door, and it was busy all day long with mainly students. But that area was also made up of business men and women and professionals including judges and lawyers.

Dad and I sat across the street every day for about a month to understand what was going on, asking ourselves the obvious question: "Why are people going *there*? And not there?"

We identified the different customers going into each establishment. The deli was all students; the café, when it was frequented by customers, seemed to be made up of more of the professional clientele. Oddly enough, when I walked into the deli, I saw an uninviting environment made up of young kids providing poor customer service, yet selling very affordable food and beverage items. The café, on the other hand, was an extremely quaint place, but with an owner who was sitting down reading the newspaper, even when customers would walk in. This created an unwelcoming environment. Therefore, we knew right away it was being run poorly.

We listed out the reasons we could succeed and analyzed costs. We were, in essence, drafting a business plan informally. At home after dinner, Dad and I sat at the table and wrote menus. Having my father with me on this venture added so much confidence and energy to my sense of security. We went through all the "What if this, what if that?" types of situations.

He would always drive home his conviction: "We can do this; *you* can do this!" and often asked, "What's the worst that could happen?" This was a very common theme with my dad.

When we identified running Coffee Caffe as a viable option, we didn't have enough capital to buy out the existing business and lease: $25,000. We needed to figure out how we were going to raise the money to do so. We reached out to a family friend, Mr. Jim Paolucci, Sr. Mr. Paolucci was a noted manufacturer of costume jewelry. He had an extremely successful business and needed a bigger location to grow. My dad selflessly found the building for him and never expected anything for his efforts. Jim Sr. could not have been more thankful, and he was the first call we made. Mr. Paolucci agreed to lend us the money, and we subsequently purchased the café business. We were able to repay Mr. P within two years! To this day, we remain very close family friends.

* * *

We'd come upon this opportunity at the right time in my father's life. Dad was fortunate to sell the homes he had built prior to the housing downturn in the 1990s, when he was in his early fifties. Due to this housing market, it was no longer advantageous to build more homes at that time after that. At the same time, as he was retiring from contracting, Dad had taken on a new passion: cooking at home. He was confident enough with his informal cooking abilities, while I was confident in my entrepreneurial skills. Given our background, and Dad's talent in the kitchen, we knew we wanted to make this an Italian-themed café. We asked ourselves, "What goes with Italian sandwiches? Soups, for sure. Pasta, definitely. Italian coffee, why not?"

After we decided on the food menu, we saw the coffee boom going crazy. I knew we had to source the best fresh-roasted beans in the area to meet customer expectations. I thought, "If we're going to attract that higher-caliber customer, we need to give them a better value."

This meant offering high-quality foods and beverages in a beautiful, comfortable place with warm and friendly employees. No shortcuts. My philosophy was always to offer a better product than the competition.

I had a sense of the market we would go after. I felt that the customer who was coming in was not going to mind paying a slightly higher price if they got a good value in return. Additionally, they weren't going to take up a table for two or three hours because they had to get back to work. We could turn the tables over quicker and generate higher revenue.

With the help of my dad, I was starting to understand a lot of the details and decisions required to grow a successful business. We had to provide a better product, so Dad made everything to order to ensure that. Yes, we were going to have to pay a premium price for ingredients, but our customers were sure to demand that. Another thing going for us was the interior of the café: it was a quaint and beautiful space constructed of all brick with working fireplaces to add to the atmosphere.

Doing the Math on Costs

The landlord knew the existing café owner would sell his business to us. He was having a problem with the rent and other costs, so he had no problem sharing with me the taxes, insurances, and all other expenses involved. When we purchased the "business" (it was not really even a business at that time), it was more of a purchase of assets and taking over an existing lease.

Next, we got intentional about menu ingredients. This part was important: we started to deeply analyze our costs here so the numbers would work long-term. We knew what a sandwich would cost; we knew the exact bakery we wanted to use for our sandwiches after tasting a *lot* of bread. There was a local bakery, Westcott Bakery, known to have the best sub roll, and we had to have it. We knew the exact cost of pasta as well. (My father would turn over in his grave today if he knew we pay six dollars a pound for organic pasta in our home). We also calculated our raw ingredient costs for pasta sauces, soups, and all the items that we had on the menu.

I did some research on local coffee roasters, so I knew what I could buy in terms of five pound bags of beans. We didn't really have to add much equipment to our balance sheet because all the equipment the previous owner had was top-of-the-line and in good condition. The espresso machine was imported from Italy. The hot coffee maker, traditional American-style, was another piece imported from Italy. All of these details went into our planning during the negotiations to purchase the business.

When we deeply analyzed all our costs, we knew what our profit margin would be in almost every category. It was concrete, and we set prices based on what we felt the market would bear and what we thought was a fair and reasonable cost to the consumer (based on the perception of the value of what we were offering). At the end of the day, we knew we had a good venture. Our ingredient costs were 5–8% lower than the industry average. We felt confident.

The one variable that wasn't predictable was our labor cost, but it was proportionate to sales as we grew. The business started with two people, my dad and myself. The labor costs went up as our revenue went up. I let the demand determine when to hire more people. We always tried to keep our growth organic and not get ahead of ourselves.

I am a math guy, a numbers guy, and we reduced our risk by knowing our numbers. Evaluating a business opportunity before starting is crucial to ensure its viability and potential for success. It will help you understand market demand, financial feasibility, and risks.

Getting the Word Out

My marketing efforts were simple: I walked around to every nearby office and handed out business cards. The idea was to tell people in the neighborhood that the café was under new ownership and talk to every front desk about what we were offering. I also listened carefully to the customers, and they became pleased with our product. For example, sometimes dedicated customers could only take a thirty-minute lunch break and couldn't feasibly drive to pick up their order and then drive back because that would eat up half of their lunch time. (We didn't have third-party food delivery platforms like DoorDash or PostMates as we do today.) Why would I take one of my staff members, during the busiest hour of the day, and drive to deliver that $40 order? I did it because I listened to the customers and their needs and then did all I could to meet those needs. The customer is always right! Cliché, but true.

We focused on serving delicious food while providing great service. Most of our customers were regulars, and I knew they needed to get to work quickly. Therefore, when I would see them pull up in the morning for their coffee, I had it waiting for them on the counter already. Obviously, that came about over time as we got to know our customers. This kind of service went a long, long way with the customer. "This is amazing" was something we heard frequently. "I'll see you at lunch!" they'd say, and, sure enough, they would come back.

The previous owner of the business did not provide this type of service. He was burned out, unmotivated, and, as a result, created an unwelcoming environment. The last thing you're going to do when you leave the office is to go into another place that makes you feel unwelcome. Because we knew service was a high priority in this business, I hired an amazing, fun-filled person to work the register. He had such a dynamic and winning personality. For example, I would often hear him say things like, "Oh my goodness, I love what you're getting today, Mrs. Smith. Joe made an amazing sandwich. Wait till you taste it! If you don't like it, I'm buying it for you." The customers loved him, and he loved the customers. Everyone left with a huge smile on their face. Never underestimate the value of customer service.

Fortunately, the café became profitable within six months.

We took the time to do what we thought would be best, and it worked out for us. Everything was taken care of in terms of the service and the quality. It made us extremely successful…represented by the lines that we had out the door. This led me to hire more and more people to continue servicing everyone to the levels that they expected. I handled the front end of the house until we got to four employees: two people took orders, one worked the register, and one worked the back. In the peak times, I went back into the kitchen with my dad because there was only so much one person could do.

The kitchen was only eighty square feet. We worked on the ends of the three-bay sink, and there was a four-burner stove on the other side. It was an extremely small workspace, but we moved through it efficiently. Everything was made fresh daily—and I mean *everything*. At five o'clock in the morning there I was, squeezing the oranges for fresh-squeezed orange juice. Dad would be beside me preparing pasta salads and starting the soup bases.

It was a lot of work. I put in twelve-hour days Monday through Friday and then approximately eight hours on Saturday. The motivation I had was simple: I wasn't going to let my dad down. This same feeling came into play later, when I joined Venice Bakery: I wasn't going to let Jimmy down. That sense of pride and those close, trustworthy relationships in business really matter.

Dad and I were a great complement to each other. It was satisfying knowing that we, as father and son, could work together so effectively. Owning and operating a business was something he wanted to do and something I wanted to do. I'd always worked with my dad to earn extra money and knew through experience that he was so easy to work with. People truly admired many things about Dad; most of all his mild-mannered generosity. As a son, that generosity was exponential. There were never disagreements or arguments. It just fit so easily and brought us both a ton of joy. Dad and I worked in the business together for about four years. Toward the end of our last year, my younger brother Peter (who was in the home improvement business with two older gentlemen who were then retiring) was trying to downsize. Though Peter had a clear knack for selling and finance, he was assisting us because we needed help.

He came in for a few hours a day to help during lunch, and my Dad and I discussed the fact that the place could only make so much in terms of revenue. We had hit the limit and didn't want to expand our hours; six to three was perfect for us, considering my dad's age and the role he played in the success of the business.

I couldn't put any more pressure on him. He was key to the success of the café because no one could cook like he could. To hire someone else for dinner was not even a consideration. I believe a successful restaurant without the owner there is almost impossible. But with a single location and not opening for dinner, there was only a finite revenue stream. As much passion as Dad had for doing this work, it was becoming a lot.

Opening another location didn't feel like the right thing to do either for all the same reasons. I thought it through and realized that with a somewhat complex menu, trying to recreate it somewhere else wasn't going to work. It wasn't like a donut shop with one simple item. This success had a lot to do with our personal commitment and involvement.

My brother and I started discussing a new venture in his industry, home improvement. I had a good manager at the café, Dennis Gallagher, who was extremely dedicated, worked hard, and knew the business through and through. When the timing was right, we sold the business to him. It worked out perfectly. Dad and I discussed the sale together, and we both felt it was the right thing to do at the right time. I agreed to finance the purchase for Dennis over two years. With a deposit and some owner financing, we made it happen. The arrangement worked out well for everyone.

7

Home Improvement & Mortgages

My brother and I started our next business with a third partner, Rocco Deluca, who brought in some valuable insight
and experience in the home improvement world. Since the
home improvement business was new to me, I took a little
bit of a backseat at first to learn from my brother. We reached
out to homeowners who needed new windows, siding, and
roofs. We went into areas where people knew their homes
needed updates and repairs, but could not afford to get
the work done. In fact, in some dire cases, their roofs were
already leaking.

Many of these homes were sixty to seventy years old,
so the need for our services was pretty clear. However, the

question was the same in nearly every household: "How do I afford it?"

This was always the pushback we heard: "I can't do it. Yes, the price is good. Yes, I would love to do this. How can you help when I do not have the money to get the work done?"

It started with the three of us doing everything. We would go out together and knock on doors in sometimes not-so-great areas. (Truthfully, It was a little bit scary at times.) What we were selling cost too much money for certain customers. Therefore, when we got pushback, we had to find some creative finance ways to help these customers. Sometimes, this consisted of asking the homeowner to help us get more business by allowing us to put up some advertising in their yards while we were doing work on their home.

We had a good sense of the value of the homes in the area, and due to the fact that most of these homes had significant equity, we could usually find the financing. At the time, many lending institutions were lending for home improvement work, especially if there was significant equity in the property. Due to my brother's experience in this business, we had direct access to those lenders, and we went to them first.

Once we got the financing approved, we'd put our signs up in their yard as we'd agreed. We had a few subcontractors who did this specific type of work, and we coordinated all the remodeling or construction accordingly. We were, in effect, a broker...which led to the startup of our second business together, a mortgage brokerage company.

We started this mortgage business because we were doing all this financial leg work but not getting compensated for having broker status. We decided if we could collect a fee for getting the financing from a lender, we'd have a second successful business. In essence, we were getting the money to pay ourselves but also helping our customers. By changing our status to that of a licensed mortgage broker, the checks arrived directly to our mortgage company from the lender.

Additionally, our awareness of the market in the area and our aggressive business approach provided us the opportunity to buy homes, do the remodeling with our subcontractors, and resell them. As you can imagine, there were a lot more revenue opportunities in the real estate and home improvement world than in running one single-location café.

We grew from three people up to eventually close to forty. Our mortgage company had a twenty-person call center in-house and a ten-to-twelve-person sales team. There was also a seven-person admin team processing all of the required paperwork.

Audition for *The Apprentice*

The reality show *The Apprentice* was extremely popular in its first year of 2004, and the prospect of competing on it was enticing to me. As with many things in my life up to that point, I thought, "Why not?"

By doing some research, I figured out what was required to audition for season two. In my townhome, I set up a camera at the end of the table and talked about my accomplishments and why I would be a good candidate to appear on the show.

I sent in my audition tape and never expected to get a call back, happy with the fact that I at least tried. A few months went by and sure enough, I got a call back!

They explained to me that this is not solely about someone's credibility or accomplishments. This is more about making an entertaining TV show."

I was like, "Okay, what does that mean?"

"We need to see more of your personality," they replied. "We need to see more of what's going to be on television, what's going to sell you. How are you with your friends when you're out? Give us something to showcase your personality."

My friends were just as excited about it as I was. We went to a local lounge, one of our regular spots, set up a tripod with a video camera rolling, and did whatever we did on a regular Friday night. Then, I had my friends film me driving to work, getting out of the car, going into the office, sitting at my desk, basically filming my entire daily routine.

The idea was the producers would see me going out, talking to friends and strangers, having a drink, and then going to work and living my life during the week as well…a full slice-of-life audition reel. I sent it all in and, unfortunately, never got a callback.

Sometimes, not everything works out the way you hope. Still, it was a fun, eye-opening, and ego-boosting little episode…much different than I expected it to be.

8

Salon & Spa

In the early to mid-2000s, I didn't want to get content with what we were doing in the mortgage business, knowing that usually every industry is cyclical. With that in mind, I wanted to hedge, to protect myself in case one business goes astray or has a dip. Thus, I went out looking for opportunities and found a struggling salon and day spa.

After doing my research as best as I could in terms of understanding the salon and spa business, I experienced a gut feeling about this industry: there would be a growing demand for higher-end salon services for men. Historically, women wanted to pamper themselves and felt very comfortable going into a salon to do so. I believed there could be a trend toward growth in the male grooming industry as well…as long as the look of the space was welcoming to them with a more masculine feel to it.

There was an opportunity to buy a distressed salon and spa in downtown Providence, just as I'd purchased the distressed café business with my dad. I saw firsthand why the business had not been doing well prior to my arrival. The staff was in chaos with what appeared to be no organization at all. The owner was not active in the business, and during multiple visits to the establishment to get a feel for the reasons why the business was failing, I witnessed the owner in the chair getting her hair done as opposed to running the business. Similar to the café environment, the salon was not an inviting place to visit. Because I knew that clients frequent these places on a regular basis, the environment should be welcoming for both new and existing clients as well.

Thus, I decided that this was a great opportunity for me to purchase the business and turn it around as I did with the café. Fortunately, it was not a lot of money, and I was able to self-fund the purchase. I negotiated sale terms with the owner and moved forward. Although my plan was to start a male-only destination, I needed to understand the business further. Thus, I ran the business as it was to get the experience necessary in the industry, keeping the assets and personnel in place. I worked with a superior design firm, LDL Studios also in Providence, that did all the drafting and the work to reimagine the space into a more upscale salon and spa for both male and female clientele.

As I was getting familiar with the business, I felt comfortable enough that I could run it even though I could not cut hair nor administer any spa services. I knew I could hire the people who could provide superior services. Thankfully, this business had the infrastructure set up already, so I didn't have to spend a lot of money on equipment or supplies. I also hired a consultant to help me understand products and fulfill my mission of providing a clear value to high-end clientele.

I started by working to identify more experienced stylists and employees. Before I terminated the ones who really weren't fitting my vision, I had to interview potential new hires to make sure I had those chairs filled. I started to reach out to a network of salon professionals to spread the word that there were some openings. I wasn't the most seasoned or experienced person in this industry when it came to interviewing, but I did the best I could in asking the right questions to see if the individual would fit.

I started interviewing for new people, and that's when I met Carla, the woman who'd eventually become my wife. Every person I hired had to perform their expert service on me. I needed to experience the service so I could feel good about marketing their individual services. As time went on, I sent in secret "shoppers." For example, my friends would go in for a massage to give me true, honest feedback. My staff knew about this: I wasn't shy about telling them this was part of our policy. Everyone knew I was serious about making ours the ultimate salon and spa in Providence County.

When I did a big reopening event, the launch was extremely successful, and it was all accomplished through networking. During this time, I went to many events for this industry. I didn't know anybody, so this was my way to introduce myself. And it didn't stop there; when I went out at night with my friends, I met the people they knew as well, an extension of their network. Thanks to all my networking and connecting, the relaunch of the salon was a great event. I immediately saw an uptick in business within ninety days of the reopening.

Marketing the salon was more challenging than marketing the café or the other businesses. We gradually increased prices by about twenty percent, which was a bit difficult for existing customers to understand. Similar to the café, I had to provide justification for this. Besides providing better services due to a more experienced staff, we created a more upscale appearance and image. The result was people were paying a little more, but we were providing more value in exchange for the higher price: giving them champagne, giving them valet parking, giving them a more talented technician. It was an uphill climb, but I was willing to stick it out and see if I could do it. The whole goal of this process was to learn about the business and then transform it into a destination for men as well as women, while evaluating the market for a male-only destination.

As time went on, the salon and spa did very well. It was a heavy cash business, and running two other businesses simultaneously created some complications. Furthermore, managing the business remotely was more difficult than I had anticipated. Fortunately, before things got too out of control, there was a great opportunity for me to sell the business to its manager, Carol Baumer. She was a hairstylist as well and was there every day overseeing operations. She was the perfect buyer due to the fact that she saw firsthand how busy we were on a daily basis and it would give her the opportunity to be an owner/operator.

The two principles that worked well for the café also worked well here. First, I bought a distressed business and turned it around. Second, I sold the business to a manager who understood the operation and saw the success of their efforts day-to-day, a person whose whole working life revolved around it. They didn't have visions of starting or running other things like I did. They were onsite every single day as working managers.

After all was said and done with the salon, I had two experiences exiting businesses in a way that was positive for everyone involved. Of course, the biggest thing for me with the salon was it introduced me to Carla.

Prior to considering Moderne Salon and Spa, I was working at a different high-end spa, basically running the hair side of the operation because we were owned by a doctor who was never there. Little by little, my friends were leaving to go work at Joe's exclusive spa. They said, "You should come join us."

I hesitated because I was in my comfort zone (and happy there), but my girlfriends were all leaving, and I was curious. So, I went into an interview with the owner. Afterward, I said, "I'm still happy where I currently work, but I will say he's cute. He's good looking."

Fast forward a couple of weeks: I took the new job.

The thing that was so attractive about Joe to me was in the middle of all the businesses he had going on, he always thought way beyond his years. For example, in that business, he was trying to eventually create an exclusive salon and spa for men. The place was amazing. It was a cool place to work, and personally, we had chemistry. A year later, we began dating, but in the meantime, I watched him run his business. He also had a mortgage company with his brother.

Then, about a year after I started working for him, Joe started having seizures. *[Ed note: you'll read about this in Chapter 10.]* It was just incredible to see how he handled that scary situation. On a Monday, I found out he needed to have surgery, but he was in the salon two days later making sure the business was okay. I was impressed by the courage he had, just to get through his health problems while still running his businesses. It was tough for me because my dad had died at forty-two years old, and Joe was that age when he had his surgery. It was pretty intense to see him fight through to the other side, to consider everything he's been through.

The thing that's clear about Joe right away is he's so smart, so intelligent. His drive is just nonstop, even now at this point in his life. And I see it in our daughter as well, the intelligence, the perfectionism. If it's not going to be 110%, Joe's not going to do it. We've built such an incredible family because of Joe being so driven. And that's one thing I so appreciate about my husband: he breaks me out of my comfort zone. He makes me a better person.

—Carla Tedeschi

9

Gold Chip Technologies

My brother's voice on the other end of the line was surprisingly calm, given the circumstances.

"The FBI is here. Everyone's got their hands up. Can you please call our attorney?"

It was a memorable moment, for sure. I almost dropped my phone.

But we're not quite there yet.

Let's rewind the story clock a little bit…

* * *

As time went on, my brother ran the mortgage company, and Rocco ran the home improvement company. We decided to start a new company registering and reselling domain names. It was hot for a minute, then kind of died out. The next big thing? Online casinos.

It started with an idea, and then the thought, "Too bad online gambling is not legal."

Through research, we found that there were very few online casinos already operating. We found that all of the existing casinos were based offshore and appeared to be in jurisdictions that legally allowed them. Thus, we realized it might be legal if we set it up on our own and ran it in a certain way. The conversation evolved: "Let's think about how we do this the right way, so we are safe."

We met with some extremely powerful and brilliant attorneys. One of them was probably one of the smartest guys I've ever met, Jim Redding. He was an international tax attorney who helped us identify the countries where this type of business was legal. We were right, and in fact, there were certain countries in the Caribbean that allowed it at the time. We settled on our location of choice, the Dominican Republic. We retained a law firm in the DR who helped us set up our high-powered servers and software there and hired the staff necessary. They also were familiar with the licensing process and helped us apply for and obtain the licenses that were needed to operate in their country.

Together with our attorneys in the U.S., we set up the necessary operation to run our cloud-based e-commerce platform. We were comfortable from a legal perspective on how we set everything up. We did not do anything unless our attorneys advised us on the proper and legal way.

Next, we purchased software from a gentleman in San Jose, California, and set up the online the casino software on the servers in the Dominican. . We ran this for four years, and it was doing extremely well, though admittedly it was not the greatest in terms of new technology and graphics and not the smoothest-running site. This was new territory at the time, to say the least. The software animation was actually quite antiquated, but it worked, more or less. Over the four years we used this software, we did not update or improve the technology, and as a result, I could see us losing customers to newer, more advanced casinos with better software.

Our competitors' sites were more interactive and fun. But ours was still a popular site, most likely because we were first to market and we had a loyal following of customers. People visited often, and we had a lot of users. Within the U.S., we were running a "cyber wallet"; within the Dominican Republic, we were running the casino. This setup was legal in their respective jurisdictions. We had 24/7 staff in the offices in Rhode Island processing credit cards for our cyber wallet company, and we had five employees in the Dominican Republic running the casino site, also alternating 24/7 shifts.

In the late nineties, we were one of the first ten online casinos. In fact, we were so early in the industry that we were part of the origination of an online casino commission. A group of us, all the owners and other industry professionals, formed an organization to advocate for the new industry.

It was rumored that the gentleman we purchased our software from in San Jose, got raided by the FBI because he was running his own online casino operation in the United States. It was rumored that part of his plea bargain was to identify others who might be doing the same thing he was doing. This may have been what set the FBI in motion.

* * *

One day, I was sitting at home in the house I was renting by the beach. We had three businesses running from the same location, and when I called the office, no one answered the phone. I called again, and again, but no one answered. I got in touch with my brother on his cell to find out why no one was answering, and he said, "The FBI is here. Everybody's got their hands up."

Oh boy. I called our lawyers. One of the attorneys rushed over there and calmed the situation down.

Next, the legal process started. Obviously, the operation had to be shut down. It did not impact the other two businesses running out of the same location (the mortgage company and the home improvement business) because they had nothing to do with it, and that was clear. We had a clear separation of businesses. In our mind, we were confident that our business was not illegal. What we were doing in the Dominican Republic was not illegal; they had gaming laws. The transactions we were processing in the U.S. were not gaming-related.

Right away, we strongly felt things would be okay, even though it would be a pain and an expensive process to defend ourselves. But we were still scared. Our lead attorney for the company suggested that each business partner get their own lawyer. There were four of us involved as owners of the online casino—myself, my brother, Rocco, and his dad. His dad was involved because in order to purchase the software we needed, which was about half a million dollars, we went out and raised the money from one of his dad's associates, so we brought Rocco's dad in as a fourth partner in exchange.

Charges were filed in three different states. The first was Rhode Island because we were all based in that state. However, after a short period of time, the state said, "There's nothing here for us. There is no casino here, no betting going on. We don't feel that this is a valid case."

The second state, Massachusetts, looked at the case and formed the same opinion Rhode Island had: *nothing happened here.* They refused to prosecute the case.

The charges were also brought in San Jose, California, because that's where the software was developed and sold from. As a result of the two other states saying no, prosecutors in California must have felt they had to take the case or dismiss it completely. They didn't dismiss it. They said, "Okay, we're going to prosecute."

* * *

We followed the advice of our corporate counsel, Mr. Redding, and each of the partners retained our own attorneys. Because I was the main person running the business, Mr. Redding recommended that I retain a lawyer in San Jose. The other partners all retained counsel in our home state of Rhode Island.

We were flying back and forth to California two, sometimes three, times a year. During those two years defending ourselves, we probably spent half a million dollars in legal fees. Although this was an exhausting and expensive two years, it was all worth it because the outcome was great: a plea bargain the attorneys struck with the court as there was not enough evidence for the state of California to take this to trial. As a result, in exchange for personal charges to be dismissed, our company agreed to pay a $50,000 fine.

We were happy to pay the fine because even though we were charged, there's no conviction on our records. At that point, it was over. But it was a stressful process and a bit scary at times. This was all new—none of us had ever been in court. Lord knows I've never been charged with anything! And there could have been federal charges on our records forever. It was something that every other casino operator in the business was watching closely. Their offshore businesses continued as there was no reason for the government to investigate them, but we were done. We would have been fine if our software developer hadn't said, "Go check out the Grand Dominican in Rhode Island."

The only thing I regret about it was where and who we bought the software from. But guess what? He was the cheapest. The other companies had significantly better software than us and are probably still operating today. I wonder, what would have happened to our operation if we had *not* opted for the cheapest option? Sometimes, the cheapest price can lead to greater costs and more problems in the long run.

* * *

Before the feds arrived that fateful day, it was extremely exciting to come in to work each morning and see what had happened overnight. We had a six-person Customer Service Call Center. When we looked at the numbers, it was like, "Oh my goodness. This is amazing."

Every day was different. Some days were better than others. I was living well at the time, going to Vegas here and there for the weekend, then flying to Miami the next weekend. I would fly to LA just for fun. This jet-setting life was a regular occurrence. Though we were doing well, an unfortunate piece of the truth is we probably didn't save for a rainy day like we should have. You don't think things are going to stop when things are going that well—because it is so easy to believe you're unstoppable.

When I look at all the businesses I started, not everything came up smelling like roses all the time, and one of my goals in writing this book is to own both the wins *and* the losses, the ups *and* the downs. Were these companies profitable enough? Sure, but it wasn't as if we knocked it out of the park on every single one. That's just unrealistic to expect from anyone. But again, all of it gave me a foundation to learn. And if you're not that good at something or not successful yet, it certainly doesn't mean you won't ever be, if my life is anything to go on. Failure often serves as a more profound teacher than success because it forces us to confront our weaknesses and reassess our strategies.

When I was making money in those businesses—the home improvement company, the mortgage company, and then the software company—everybody knew. We were big fish in a small pond. Egotistically, I did start to think I was somewhat invincible and began taking on these additional risks, which I would never do today. I believe my brain tumor, which you'll read about in the next chapter, was a sign from above: *slow down!*

10

A Major Setback

Very few people have the experience of waking up in a hospital bed on a Sunday with no idea how or why they got there.

I am one of them.

Let's back up.

When I started having seizures, I didn't know what was happening because I was living on my own, and the seizures were nocturnal—they occurred only when I was sleeping. Also, I couldn't see myself very clearly. When I woke up in the morning, I was still in a fog. I didn't know I had rashes all over me; I didn't know I looked as bad as I did. As I explained in the previous chapter, 2006 Joe wasn't living a happy, healthy life. He was out partying, traveling weekends, flying back and forth to California to party for two nights, and so forth and so on. That lifestyle, and my history of sports with a few concussions, is what I believe led to my brain tumor.

* * *

I woke up one day with the entire side of my body paralyzed. I also had a full rash on my body, completely *red*. I drove myself to the walk-in clinic to figure out what the heck was going on. At any walk-in clinic, you'll usually experience a lot of waiting, both out in the lobby and also once they finally call you back. This was not the case with me that day.

As I checked in, the front desk attendant immediately said, "Come with me." I did not know what was happening, but they took me right into the doctor's office, did all these tests on me, and ultimately felt it was some sort of skin rash. They sent me home.

Two weeks later, again I woke up with the same symptoms. This time, I went to my doctor's office located in a large medical facility. He was concerned and took me across the hall to the dermatologist. They did some scans, but again, there was no diagnosis.

A couple of weeks later, I woke up with blood all over me. I had actually bit right through my tongue. I got nervous because I saw blood, so I called my mother, she came right over, and we called 911. The paramedics rushed me to the hospital.

Mom made my doctor aware of what had happened, and he ordered an MRI immediately. That's when they finally discovered the tumor in my brain, specifically a meningioma. It was above and behind one of my eyes in the frontal lobe. This was on a Sunday in January of 2007; surgery was scheduled immediately for Friday morning of that week. I certainly wasn't thinking about the potential negative outcomes of the surgery. I just thought, "If this is what my doctor is saying that I must do, let's go."

During those five days while waiting for surgery, I was not preparing for the worst. I had no time to think about what could happen under the knife. I was more concerned with, "Is my mortgage paid? Is my car note paid? Are all my bills paid? Is the business going to be okay?" I was actually more concerned about my responsibilities than the worst outcome possible from such a major medical procedure.

My sister Susan came over, and we went to dinner the night before the surgery. She probably sensed the seriousness of the situation more than I did, though I started to feel the severity of the situation and got quite anxious that Thursday night. She stayed with me at my place; surgery was scheduled for Friday morning at 6:30 a.m., the first surgery of the day. The operation was performed at Roger Williams Hospital by one of the leading neurosurgeons in the state, Dr. Prakash Sampath. When I arrived at the hospital at 5:00 a.m. for the prep, my family was all there, and I remember them being with me prior to the nurses rolling me into the operating room.

I believe the surgery lasted a few hours, and then I woke up in the hospital room with my family still there, surrounding me on each side of the bed. The tumor was determined to be benign. Fortunately, I was blessed that the surgeon didn't have a bad day.

I had forty-two staples in my head, was bandaged up in a turban-like wrap, and was feeling quite groggy. The doctor came in minutes later and assured me that the procedure went great. They started me immediately on anti-seizure meds; however, I again started to break out in a rash. Of course, terrible thoughts went through my head. Once the nurses came in and saw this, they stated that this rash was probably a result of an allergic reaction to one particular drug, so they started me on a second. Sure enough, this was it.

After several hours of recovery, the doctor and nurses were seriously considering sending me home the next day! After further discussion with the team, they all decided it would be best for me to stay two days for close monitoring. To me, that was still *quick.* I was shocked. I could not believe they would be discharging me less than forty-eight hours after having brain surgery, but I was glad they did! There was no better place than home that I wanted to be.

Once I went home (or, rather, to my parents' house so they could keep an eye on me), my close family members and friends visited. Admittedly, I was a little reluctant about this due to my condition. It was a very humbling experience. After the surgery, I remember talking to a radiologist who said, "You're going to be fine. You're not going to have seizures anymore." He was correct in the fact that there was no tumor left, but he was not correct when he said I'd never have another seizure.

There was a recovery period of probably four weeks when I was not able to do anything but rest. I was fortunate: there was no need for rehab after surgery because I hadn't lost any functioning. I had to go back and forth to the doctor's office during that time and eventually got the staples across my head removed. I took it easy for about four to six weeks before eventually going back to work at the mortgage company on a part-time basis.

I started to feel more like myself and, as a result, began to go out a bit again in March. Incredibly, all I had been through didn't stop me from partying. I was feeling confident again. But six weeks later, guess what happened?

* * *

It was a Friday night in April. I went out, not knowing (not accepting) my restrictions. I partied that night, and then went into the office the next day. It was just me and my brother in the office, and on his way out, he came to say goodbye. That's when he discovered me on the floor. He called 911, and I woke up the next day in the hospital with no idea about what had happened or how I'd gotten there.

Apparently, I suffered five grand mal seizures between Saturday and the time that I woke up on Sunday. A grand mal seizure is a whole-body seizure, with no warning ahead of time—no aura, no sense they're coming. Previously, my seizures were all nocturnal, and as a result of not taking proper care of myself after the surgery, I opened some of the staples in my head by falling on the floor. Doctors were concerned about an infection. Dr. Sampath felt that the safest thing to do would be to reopen my sutures to fix everything, but that procedure wasn't scheduled for six weeks later. This time was much worse mentally than the first surgery because I now had time to think about things. It was an emotional time, and even today, reflecting on it is tough.

Because the first surgery was scheduled so quickly, it was like, "You have to do this," and I didn't think about the outcome. All I thought about was, "What do I need to do to get ready for this?" I had no time to think about the consequences; it was more my responsibilities I was concerned about.

The second surgery was scheduled for June. I had lots of visits with the doctor and my neurologist before the day, and we discussed the procedure in depth—including how things would have to change in my life. They explained to me what I had to do and how my life had to be altered in order to minimize these seizures. I had to stop drinking. I had to stop staying out late at night. I had to try to minimize my stress levels and get lots of sleep. Because this was not an invasive surgery (comparatively speaking) and more of a "clean up," my confidence level was up that morning in June of 2007. Mom and Dad drove me to the hospital early in the morning as they did in January, and stayed by my side until the medical staff took me into the operating room. When I woke a few hours later, they were by my side again. The doctor was also there, reassuring me that this procedure was again successful and I would be fine. I was remarkably discharged later that day.

* * *

After the second surgery, I was definitely going to follow doctors' orders and take time off. During this time I didn't have much of a social life, and I wasn't working. My new lifestyle had to begin immediately, and I became much more conscious about preventing potential seizures. No more drinking, no more partying, no more jet-setting. When I thought about the alternative, it was easy to adapt to this. Of course, there was a short period of time when I asked, "Why me?" and "What did I do to deserve this?" I rested for a big part of that time. I would get together with friends for dinner and they would visit me at home, but the lifestyle I was used to was definitely over.

I was also out of the businesses I'd shared with my brother and Rocco. I was living off my GMAC 401k savings and my personal savings accounts, and collecting Social Security disability just to get by. I was doing anything and everything I could to pay for my mortgage and my car. It was definitely one of the lowest points of my life in many ways.

I could not work, yet I couldn't *not* work and expect my money to last forever. I had to figure out what I was going to do. After a year and a half, I went on interviews regardless of whether they were for jobs I really wanted to do or not. I was just hoping to land a job to collect a paycheck. The rejection I encountered from those experiences was eye-opening and humbling for me. These were for jobs I knew would not be huge challenges for me, such as a local bank's financial analyst. This was not going to be tough for me based on my confidence level and my ability at that point, but no one would give me the chance to do it. I had always been an entrepreneur up to that point, so trying to go back into the corporate world just to get a paycheck was not going to work. So, instead of focusing on what I could not do, I asked, "What else *can* I do?"

Then, I had a notion. I thought about all of the customers I helped get mortgages and refinance their homes during the housing boom in the early 2000s while I had the mortgage company. Now that the housing crisis had hit, I thought about how I could help these customers who were in dire need of some assistance. Thus, I created a small loan modification business out of my house, helping under-water mortgage holders adjust their terms. This was one solution, one thing I could realistically do and do well. It paid my bills, but not much more. My intuition and hustle kicked in when I recognized the weight of my financial responsibilities, driving me to seek creative solutions such as this new venture. This unwavering determination ensured that I could pay my bills and give me the stability that was needed for me at that time.

* * *

Unfortunately, I still do have "breakthrough" seizures every three to four years; I see my neurologist and do MRIs once a year. There's no indication of any tumor, just scar tissue. In the neurology world, that's fantastic. But to me, even one seizure is awful. When one does occur today, I can usually look back and attribute it to a stressful time or to a stretch of poor sleep.

The aftermath of the breakthrough seizures I experience is overwhelming to me. My body gets extremely tense, and I am sore for at least two to four weeks. My exercise routine feels like I am starting all over again, and my mental state gets confused and cloudy for at least two weeks. My trainer says it takes me a good month to get back to where I was before a seizure. It's very emotional, and I feel deeply sad for my loved ones and those who care for me, especially Carla who witnesses the physical effects of me going through seizures. Although I know it's not my fault,

I really hate putting anyone through it. It is something I unfortunately have to live with every day, and I truly would not wish this upon anyone. Once I am able to think about things a little clearer, I realize I cannot let it bring *me* down.

Before we move on to the next part of my story, I want to take a moment here to emphasize that I felt as if I was at rock bottom during this time in my life after my second brain surgery. Not only was recovering from my brain tumor a significant mental setback, but it was such a financial setback as well.

At this time I was living in my townhome in East Greenwich, Rhode Island, and burning through my savings and my 401k. In 2009, I felt desperate. I was struggling in many ways to find a solution, to keep going. I knew the hurdles I had to overcome physically. But I also had that hurdle of just plain *surviving* as well.

"How am I going to pay my bills? What if I can't afford my bills? Who's going to want to hire me at this stage of my life, in this mental state?"

This is a small sampling of a lot of things that were going through my mind. I really was not sure where the outcome would be. It wasn't like I could go to my parents and start asking for money to pay my bills. They were always supportive of me in so many countless ways, but now I had to figure this out.

I also had some great friends who truly understood what I was going through in those years. One friend stands out in my mind as I reflect on this part of my life. His name was Steve Marra, a very successful restaurateur in the state. He was always there for me; he understood my financial situation and was very generous when we went out together. We lived close to each other, so it was easy for him to pick me up and drop me off when we went out. His willingness to do that, to include me in that way, meant a lot.

Another good friend of mine growing up who I hung out with a lot during that period (and one who I'm still friends with today) was Jimmy Paolucci, who is the son of Mr James Paolucci. Jimmy and his brother Gino rented a house in Newport, Rhode Island, every summer and invited me to come down and stay. They never asked anything of me, even though I stayed there frequently. Obviously, they understood my position as well. Truly great friends.

I had a lot of friends like this, and their presence in my life helped me with the confidence to continue—to not fall into a depressed state. This time was difficult in many ways, but when setbacks like this happen in life, I learned that you find ways to get through it…and that a huge part of that process, for me, was the fact that I didn't have to do it alone, thanks to my generous friends and Carla's unconditional support throughout. We're human beings, and sometimes we fall and we need help. Accept that help and be that help for others in return when you can.

Mentally bouncing back after hitting rock bottom required me to shift my perspective entirely. I had to embrace the fact that failure wasn't a dead end, but a stepping stone. Although I felt the pain in many ways, I couldn't dwell on it. I focused on what I could control: my mindset, which was always my strength.

Things *will* turn around. In my case, it happened when the phone rang one day. My old friend Jimmy, out in California, needed help with his family business.

11

Pizza!

Give them quality. That's the
best kind of advertising.
—Milton S. Hershey

Venice Bakery was a three-generation family-owned business, a food manufacturer specializing in artisanal bread and baked goods. They offered a wide range of products and catered to various industries such as food service, retail, and hospitality. Known for high-quality ingredients, traditional baking methods, and commitment to sustainability, Venice

Bakery also offered custom product development and private labeling services.

It was started by my business partner Jimmy's grandfather and grandfather's brother, both of whom emigrated to the United States from Italy. Originally settling in the Bronx, New York, in 1930, the brothers founded Palmeri Pizza Crust Company and started making wheat-based pizza dough. After a few years, they packed up their families and drove across the country to Venice Beach, California, to enjoy a climate similar to their Sicilian home in Pioppo. The business they purchased there in 1953, Venice Bakery, became known as the Venice Baking Company.

After four years, the brothers bought an 11,000-square-foot building ten miles south in El Segundo, California, where the business continued their manufacturing. They sold dough to local bakeries, local restaurants, and some food service establishments through distribution. Over the years, Jimmy's father ended up joining the business, as did Jimmy and his brother Larry later on. Eying an opportunity to grow the operation, Jimmy ended up buying out his brother at the same time his father retired.

During this time, Jimmy met with a holistic physician at the University of Southern California, Dr. Karima Hirani, who worked with autistic children. She asked Jimmy if he could make an allergen-free, gluten-free pizza since she had found improved behavioral patterns in the children she worked with when they were eating a gluten-free diet.

Now with complete autonomy to run the business his way, Jimmy's interest was piqued, and he took on the challenge. With the help of an insightful raw material representative, Trish Dozier, they went to work to fulfill Dr. Hirani's request. At the time, Venice Bakery was making only wheat-based products, so Jimmy worked on this project during the off times: weekends, nights, early mornings. He went in and mixed up batches of formulations, experimenting with different ratios of ingredients. Together with Ms. Dozier, Jimmy was able to come up with the perfect gluten-free dough formulation that sang. One year later, a new pizza crust in a completely new food product category was made! It was revolutionary!

It was not intended to be a commercial product; it was developed in the hopes of helping children. But there was something special about it. As he was giving his new pizza crusts out to some friends in the area with children who had behavioral issues, they kept coming back and requesting more. He thought, "Wow. You know, maybe we have something here."

At this time, I was still back in Rhode Island, recovering from my brain surgery while reentering the workforce by starting up my loan modification business. It was the perfect time for me to get into something new and exciting: selling an unproven pizza product on the East Coast.

Of the decision to see if I could help his business in those early years, Jimmy recently said, "I did have many business contacts in the pizza business and in LA, but my decision to call Joe was based on the long-term relationship we'd had by then, the trust factor, the business sense, etc. Joe's intelligence and business experience, with me out on the front line, was the dynamic duo recipe for success. Yes, he had a string of bad luck with the brain tumor and seizures that followed, but I never doubted his ability. This was the opportunity to get him back in the game."

Extremely grateful for this opportunity and trust, I said, "Let me see what I can do with this." As you probably concluded by now, new opportunities have never felt threatening to me; instead, they ignite a sense of excitement. Challenges embraced with enthusiasm are opportunities for me to grow and achieve more. This has been the story of my life.

* * *

I began cold-calling pizzerias, restaurants, supermarkets, and any other potential buyers from my home. As you might imagine, I was met with endless rejection. No one knew what "gluten-free" even was, or why anyone would want it. No one understood the celiac and gluten-intolerant populations and the opportunity that offering something different could bring to their food establishment. It was a difficult task breaking through, to say the least. Finally, I got the attention of an interested group, Duane Reade.

Based in New York and owned by Walgreens, Duane Reade is the largest and most recognized full-service drug store in New York City. They offer all types of services and products, from medical supplies to groceries.

Having generated a sincere interest, I was tasked with selling them on the importance of offering a gluten-free pizza even though it was an unproven market (and I had limited sales experience outside of my own small businesses). Over a few months, I educated the buyers at Duane Reade on the celiac and gluten-intolerant market and how it was important to have a gluten-free product in their stores. Once they were sold on the opportunity, my next task was to convince them our product was the best and only option to consider.

To do this, Jimmy overnighted the frozen crusts to Rhode Island. I then packed them up with cans of pizza sauce, cheese, and a portable pizza oven. Next, I got on the train for a three-hour trek to NYC, wheeling coolers filled with everything I needed down the streets of New York. The buyers were waiting for me, and I cooked up pizzas for the staff during their lunch break and waited for what I hoped would be only positive feedback. Although the feedback on the taste couldn't have been better, it was still difficult for the buyers to understand the bigger picture and take a risk on this product. I went back and forth to New York City doing the same exercise twice a week for about four weeks.

Finally, they agreed to allow us to test the product in a new store opening. My persistence and grit paid off.

They gave me the date of the opening, and I started getting ready with Carla's help. Stocking a store was much different than bringing a few pizzas up on the train and cooking for an office.

I set up an assembly line to put the pizzas together in Rhode Island so we could meet the given timeline for our East Coast debut. I went to a local PIP printer and had the labels printed for the top of the pizzas while my friend Steve helped me put together a team of six people in line to top the pizzas with sauce and cheese. We then had to shrink wrap the finished topped pizzas using hair dryers, put them in coolers full of ice, and drive three hours to New York City the night before the new store opening.

Carla knew this was a big and important moment in my attempt to show Jimmy just how much I could accomplish in such a short time, so she left work early to take the trip with me. We needed to get into the store before 12:00 a.m. since the cleaning people were not allowed to let anyone in after midnight. As anyone who has driven to or from New York City knows, the traffic can be crazy. Sure enough, we were late. We were frantically running up and down the streets of New York City looking for the store while pulling the coolers behind us…and it was now 12:30 a.m.!

When we found the store, I started knocking on the glass windows, trying to get the attention of anyone who may be inside. The cleaning people finally saw us and fortunately let us in as I explained to them why we were there. Carla and I loaded up the pizzas in the deli case and drove three hours back to Rhode Island in the early hours of the morning.

Whew. It was my first account for Venice Bakery, and it was certainly a memorable one. Overcoming the obstacles of educating new customers on a new, untested product was a stepping stone toward my future success.

12

A Handshake
& A Side Desk

Addressing the challenges of getting a gluten-free pizza product to Winn-Dixie, one of the largest supermarkets in the southeastern part of the U.S., was formidable. Again, this was not an easy sell due to the infancy of the gluten-free market. I wasn't great with PowerPoint in those days, but I did the best I could in terms of presentation, supporting the gluten-free market and our product with data. They came back and asked for a lot of relevant details about the product and about the quality assurances behind it.

Venice Bakery did not yet have a dedicated quality assurance (QA) department at that time. Remember, Jimmy was running the business with approximately fifty people, selling regular wheat-based dough. This gluten-free category was unknown at that time (this would soon change). Therefore, figuring out how to devote the proper resources and attention to this new and fair request by Winn-Dixie was a little bit of a challenge.

Venice Bakery was producing both wheat-based and gluten-free pizza crust on the same manufacturing line to start. We ran wheat-based products from Monday afternoon through Saturday, then shut down on Sunday while a team of employees came in to spray down the equipment, sanitize, clean the floors, wipe down the walls, and change up the equipment—whatever we needed to do to make sure we were using dedicated equipment for gluten-free products as opposed to wheat-based products. On Monday mornings, we started up with gluten-free manufacturing on a clean, sanitized production line and ran until the orders were filled—then got back into our regular wheat-based manufacturing. We followed this protocol to eliminate cross-contamination.

I was able to convey our level of commitment to the buyers, which gave these earliest customers the comfort level they needed. We took responsibility for any cross-contamination issues as well. Finally, we provided any and all customers with gluten tests for every production run. These gluten test kits were administered in-house to make sure our products tested below five parts per million. (The FDA mandated twenty parts per million to qualify a product to be gluten-free, but we held ourselves to a stricter standard.)

Once we loaded the product on the distributor's truck and it left our facility, it was no longer our responsibility because we didn't know what was going to happen to that product after it left our building.

We had very high standards internally, and we went above and beyond to uphold them. With this level of safety and assurances, our customers were very comfortable. After presenting them with several data points around the market demand and opportunity, we were given the opportunity to launch in their markets.

Winn-Dixie owns a number of stores. However, like many large grocery store chains, they did test cases in a regional area first—in this case, it was the southeast region. Our product was well-received there, and, as a result, they now started to place purchase orders.

This was an *enormous* win for Venice Bakery.

* * *

I saw my efforts as proof of my abilities. There was no compensation for the work that I had done up to this point. However, after the Winn-Dixie account was established, Jimmy and I agreed that to really help expand the business, I would need to relocate to California.

I sat down with my parents and said, "I have an opportunity to go to work in California with Jimmy. I know you guys are getting older, but I think this could be a good thing for me. I will only be a six-hour flight away and Susan is close by, but I want to be sure that I have your blessing."

Mom replied, "Joey, if you can go out there and better yourself, do it. We're not going to stop you. Don't hold back because of us."

Their blessing meant a lot to me since I had to move to California to fulfill every opportunity, to grow, and to answer all the what-ifs. I had to seize the opportunity presented to me by Jimmy because I knew I could do more than what I was doing in Rhode Island. I was in an unfortunate situation that was impacting my career path. Living off of my savings, IRAs, and Social Security was not sustainable. My future was in California. I felt that I had nothing to lose. I did not want my biggest regret to be the chance I never took.

The physical separation from my parents was the hardest part of leaving the East Coast. However, things worked out, as you will read about, so I am now in a position to help my mom out. I say my mom because, unfortunately, my dad suffered from Parkinson's disease, Alzheimer's, and dementia during the last five years of his life. It was a tough time for my mom having to care for him every day, even though she had a caretaker come in three times a week to help. My sister Susan was also a big help and offered any and all the assistance she could.

My dad passed away in 2018, six weeks after my daughter Audrey was born. The passing of my dad was devastating to me. I no longer had that person that I could call every day for guidance; I no longer had that person that could lift me up when I was down or feeling like life was just not fair. He was my inspiration. This was a time of reality that I was now the patriarch to the legacy that he left behind, while also needing to step up and try to raise a family on my own with responsibilities that he instilled in me.

Carla and I also talked it over. We were a solid couple by then, but my future in California was not yet a sure thing. Although my gut told me this was the right move, it was risky. We agreed I'd go on my own for a year, and she'd join me if things looked good after twelve months.

* * *

In October 2010, I sold my townhouse in Rhode Island in a short sale, sold all of my furniture, and moved out West. I eventually became President of Venice Bakery. (Jimmy was the CEO.)

"I used to do everything when it came to going out and selling the products to the customer," Jimmy said recently as we were reflecting on our history. "All the different line items they were going to need, looking at our costs, pricing those line items. I turned all that over to Joe. I would let the customer know, 'Okay, we're going to get back to you within three days. We'll have all the pricing and everything set up so you can understand what it's going to look like to the distributor and from the distributor to you.'

"After Joe came out, I didn't have to deal with that anymore. And he was able to always tick everything a notch higher to create more profitability for the company."

One of the reasons we complemented each other so well was that Jimmy was the face of the company. He loved networking, going out to bring in new customers. I didn't excel at those things; I was more of an operations person tasked with figuring out the answers to questions like, *How can we increase profitability in an efficient manner? How do we execute on fulfilling larger and larger orders? How are we going to scale production as we continue to grow?*

In the beginning, we organically developed our roles. I like to use the truck going down the road analogy. Jimmy had his foot on the gas pedal, while I made sure we stayed on the road. He saw the benefit I could add to the business, and he knew his own value in terms of going out there and getting more business in this category that was ready to explode. My presence helped Jimmy focus on the vision while I focused on the operations.

"There was no doubt in my mind that Joe was the right call when it became clear this thing, this new product, was going to *go*," Jimmy said. "He was exactly the person I needed to make this thing work on the inside. Anybody who meets Joey knows he's probably one of the smartest guys you'll ever meet on the planet. When it comes to organization, and making tough decisions, he's the guy you want. Nobody else even came to mind."

* * *

Since the gluten-free pizza category was new and still unproven, it represented a small fraction of Venice Bakery's overall revenue in 2011.

When I came out to California to help Jimmy, $70,000 was the salary offer. I didn't really even have a job title. It was more like, "I need your help. I can pay you this amount to start, get you an apartment, and get you a car." We both knew it wasn't much; however, it gave me an opportunity to show what I could do.

The thought of living with potential seizures still haunted me every day, but I felt like I had them under control when I returned to California. Nevertheless, those breakthrough seizures (which, to this day, happen every three to four years) do set me back. But as we continued to see positive results in the new food category, we were energized. And there was no way I was going to let Jimmy down, just like I hadn't wanted to let my dad down when we embarked on our café business back in the late eighties. It was always my unwavering commitment—and the loyalty I felt to those who believed in me—that kept me going. Especially when the stakes were high.

I was working from the corner of Jimmy's desk when I first started. In 2012, we negotiated an equity stake for me and became formal business partners, which you'll read about in the following chapters. Jimmy is one of the most generous men I know, and we have a great relationship. From the beginning, our deals were all made by handshake.

These relationships are far and few between. It is not easy to find a partner that you bond with, complement each other's talents, and are best friends. It truly is remarkable. We worked beautifully together as business partners. In fact, we still have all of our investments together, and we review new opportunities as a team.

* * *

A tragedy occurred not long after my arrival in California. I share it here (with Jimmy's permission) as an example of how he and I were able to be there for each other. Jimmy's older brother, an active surfer who was married with two wonderful children in Huntington Beach, passed away unexpectedly from a lung clot. There are no words that can properly express how extremely tragic and completely unexpected this loss was for everyone. Jimmy was, of course, devastated.

I had suffered my brain tumor just a few years prior and experienced a great deal of difficulty getting back on my feet. In the wake of my situation, as you have read, Jimmy invited me to come out to California to help him. Jimmy had been there for me; he'd given me an opportunity at the right time...when I really needed one. Then, while he was suffering through the loss of his brother, I was there for him while he took time to deal with his grief and be there for his family. Two years later, Jimmy went through a difficult divorce. During that time, he was suffering and distracted from the day-to-day operation of Venice Bakery. Sometimes, he'd call me in the early hours of the morning and ask me to take a ride to the beach to talk. I was more than happy to be there for him. We were there for each other... and we still are.

In life, in business, and in relationships, there can be no limit (and no guarantees) in terms of what it takes to create something special. When you're all in, you've made it clear you won't hold anything back. You're there for the 3:00 a.m. call. You're there for the twelve-hour shift.

Loyalty to your business partner is one of the most crucial elements of success. It's the foundation of trust, which is essential for navigating the challenges and uncertainties in business. When both partners are committed to each other, they create a strong bond that can weather any storm, making the business stronger and more resilient.

Originally, my brother and I ran the family business together, but he had two kids and was reluctant to take risks. We all have different thresholds for risk depending on where we are in our lives. When we don't have anything, our threshold is high. But when you have kids or a lot of money, your threshold for risk is low.

We were just in different places in our lives, so I went to my brother and said, "Listen, I want to go out and take risks and do things, and you don't want to. So, let's do an evaluation of the business. And then you can either buy me out or I'll buy you out…let's go our separate ways. One of us could just run the business as we want and not create a whole lot of friction in our relationship."

Ultimately, I ended up buying my brother out of the business before gluten-free was even a thought. As for Joe, there was no way this business was going to run with just one of us there. We needed both, and we knew the roles we were going to play.

I needed somebody inside running things, someone who was going to watch all aspects. One of the hardest things to do when you're growing as fast as we were growing is to find the right people to put in the right positions to run your different departments. We had to go through many people…and in some positions, we never really found the right fit. They got us by.

As for making Joe my business partner, it was just the right thing to do. The right thing to do is *never to be greedy when you're running a business*. When you're greedy, you might succeed in the short term, but you're never going to succeed long term. It was definitely the right thing to do to let Joe know he had ownership in this company as well.

I lost my older brother when he was 47. Joe and I, we pull each other through tough times. Thank God he came to LA to save me when my string of bad luck hit. Losing my only brother and managing a horrible divorce took my eye off the ball, but Joe was focused. Joe was there. But I was there for him, too, after his brain tumor when he needed an opportunity. We were there for each other.

That kind of struggle gives you a bulletproof vest. Like, what else could possibly happen? When you have these traumatic events in your life, and you've fought through them and landed back on your feet? After that, you are ready to go. You're ready to tackle anything.

There was never a time when I felt the decision to bring Joe into the business was wrong. I never regretted the decision. There was never a bump in the road that made either of us question the decision. There was too much going on as fast as the business was growing. Managing accounts, purchasing another building, setting up more manufacturing lines, growing the distribution network, hiring the right people to run the different departments—the business was on our minds twenty-four hours a day, seven days a week.

—Jimmy DeSisto

13

Doing The Math...Again

The original Venice Bakery plant was small; our manufacturing footprint was only about 6,000 square feet. The line
started with a mixer. Employees tossed fifty-pound bags of
flour in with sugar, yeast, and other dry and wet ingredients.
Most bakers know the process, yet all products and companies have slight differences. This was an old-school operation
and required a lot of labor. We probably had twenty-five to
thirty people on the line in the original factory.

Jimmy knew a lot about the process of making pizza...
in-depth details about how different ingredients would
interact with others. I didn't grow up in that world. When
it came to the details of the dough-making process, Jimmy
was much more in tune with its rhythms than I was. He also

knew everybody working at Venice; they knew his dad and his brother. It was like an extended family to many of them.

You can imagine, then, how well people took it when I came in from the outside, working right away in a leadership capacity. Jimmy brings in some guy who looks like he's trying to take over? I wasn't the most popular person in the earliest days after I joined the company...I had to make sure I was treading lightly to some degree. I did not want to come across as knowing everything and being the best, so instead I tried to make everyone else better.

"It takes time to build relationships with anybody," Jimmy said, remembering those years. "A leadership role comes with a level of power *and* the challenges of having to make some hard decisions." For example, when you have somebody running a department who is proving to not be the right person, it's a pretty hard thing to say, "This isn't working out. We're not going to let you go, but we *are* going to change your responsibilities now, and you're going to have to report to someone."

Personnel issues—whether a transition in roles or even a termination—could be challenging. Terminating a long-time employee is one of the most difficult decisions to make as a leader. It's a mix of sadness and responsibility, knowing that you're not just ending a job for someone, but affecting someone's livelihood. Venice was a family, so these decisions were even harder. Even if you know it's the right choice for the business, it doesn't ease the pain of letting go of someone who has been a loyal part of the company.

"Those were decisions Joe made," Jimmy said. "He was responsible for finding people to head up departments, whether it was shipping and receiving, quality control, plant managers, or production managers. Maintenance was always such a challenge—trying to find the right guys to be able to maintain equipment, especially with the older style of dough press equipment we used. And then new, updated equipment came in as well, as we built out our 60,000-square-foot facility later on. I don't care how new or old anything is, when it's running twenty-four hours a day, it better be maintained and have clean oils running through it as well as working cooling systems. Still, things are going to break. Anything with moving parts is going to break."

It wasn't easy all of the time, yet today, when I go back to visit the factory, there's a lot of warmth and a lot of love. It's a reminder that while people don't take well to change initially, they get used to it, especially if the change is positive! (And I like to think my efforts at Venice were ultimately good for everyone there.)

My role was to grow the company from the inside out—the infrastructure and the big-picture operation of it. For example, as we continued our fast-paced growth, there was a clear need for a qualified, experienced plant manager. At first, that job was done by Jimmy himself. He was running down to the line from the office to answer questions or fix processes—constantly.

Meanwhile, I was upstairs thinking, "We can't operate this way forever. Jimmy can't be running up and down the stairs, and I simply don't know enough yet about the nuances of this manufacturing process."

Though I didn't have pizza-making in my blood like Jimmy, I had a lot of practical business sense based on my years of entrepreneurship. I focused on the operations, on the marketing, and on the numbers. As I looked at the dollars and cents of selling pizza crusts, I did the math just like I had back in the day at Coffee Caffe. We already had Jimmy's excellent gluten-free formulation and a unique process for getting it made, and it was obvious that there were more opportunities in selling a gluten-free pizza crust for $1.35 per unit than a wheat-based unit for $0.25.

There was no more labor involved in creating this higher-priced product. The fixed costs basically stayed the same, regardless of whether we devoted our efforts to regular wheat-based dough or gluten-free dough. The only thing we were increasing with the latter was our raw material costs. Therefore, our margins went from low-digit percentages to an EBITDA (earnings before interest, taxes, depreciation, and amortization) of over 35% when we sold the business in 2017—an astronomical number in this industry.

* * *

I have to reiterate this piece because it made all the difference in the trajectory of the company: we were pricing our product at the market rate, yet when you compare what we were producing with what we used to produce we were *five times higher* profit-wise with no increase in labor and no increase in fixed overhead, just a variable cost increase in our ingredients. It was a no-brainer for us to start reducing our wheat-based side of the business and just focus our efforts on gluten-free crusts." Evaluating profit margins is critical in making informed strategic business decisions, especially in growing a company. It allows you to understand the true financial health of your business and identify areas where costs can be optimized. I knew that by regularly analyzing profit margins, you can make informed data-driven decisions that contribute to the company's long-term success.

It worked out. Our foresight about moving more fully into gluten-free products was obviously correct. As we grew our gluten-free sales, however, it was important for us to be honest about who *exactly* our product was for. We had flour all over the place in our production facility. It was on the ground and it was in the air, despite our careful weekly sanitation efforts. We helped our customers with disclaimers for their customers to understand the sensitivity of allergens that read: "Gluten-free pizza is not intended for true celiacs. It is made in a facility that processes wheat." Once we started manufacturing in our new building, this disclaimer was not necessary, as the part of the building that made gluten-free crusts was a dedicated gluten-free area.

Joe moved to California, and I stayed back. I was a little bit scared to move because we weren't engaged; we weren't married. We were just dating at that point. I also was financially supporting my mom, who spoke no English. I had supported her since my dad passed away. It was hard for me to make the decision to move, but I always said, "If it's meant to be, it will be."

After Joe moved to California, he made it a point, once a month, to fly me out there. We did that for one year, and every month, there was so much growth in both of us. My mom saw it and would never have stopped me from going. She was so happy; she adored my husband.

Prior to that year, Joe had encouraged me to create my own business. He set me up with my LLC and introduced me to his financial people, including his accountant, Ed Restivo. Once when Joe was already out in California and it was tax season, our accountant asked me, "What are you still doing here? Why are you not in California?"

I said my usual line, "If it's meant to be, it will be."

He said, "The best decision Joe ever made for himself was to leave Rhode Island. This state is way too small for him. The way that man thinks, he had to leave to go to a bigger playing field."

I understood what the accountant meant. Even today, when it comes to people who manage his finances, Joe will pay close attention and then ask pointed questions. It's not uncommon for one of the professionals to respond, "Ha, I never thought about it like that."

His brain just never stops. He's always ten steps ahead; always looking at things from different angles, and thinking about others first. Sometimes I wish he'd think about himself first! But his dad was such a kind soul, so I really believe Joe gets a lot of his goodness from him. Joe Sr. was such a good, good man.

—Carla Tedeschi

In one short year, we saw some drastic growth we never expected—not that quickly, anyway. At the end of 2011, things seemed like the trajectory was headed in the right direction. Carla and I talked. We talked about our relationship, our future, and our lives. Carla knew that the best opportunities for me to continue to thrive were in California and with Venice Bakery.

Carla then moved out here officially in January of 2012, and we got engaged at Lake Como in Italy, which you'll read about in Chapter 16. We were married here in California in 2013 and have been enjoying each other, Audrey, and our family deeply ever since.

14

Venice Bakery IP & National Distribution

While other manufacturers may have done the analysis I discussed in the previous chapter as well, they didn't have the infrastructure we were blessed to have. Our intellectual property, our gluten-free formulation, and our unique process of being able to scale quickly in bulk were the differentiators.

When I arrived in California in October of 2010, Venice Bakery was operating three to five days a week, eight hours per day, due to the focus on wheat-based pizza and the core customers of the company, which were schools. This resulted in a decline in demand during the summer months.

Again, our move into a gluten-free product made all the difference. When Venice Bakery was making dough and pizza the way everybody made pizza, it was being made on the same equipment Jimmy's grandfather had used. The competition and the bigger companies like Nestlé, Schwan's, and Domino's were using newer state-of-the-art, multimillion-dollar lines of pizza-making equipment. The newest equipment, which stretched the dough and cut it at a high speed, was extremely efficient and didn't require a lot of labor. But the thing is, gluten holds ingredients together; it's what gives the dough elasticity. Thus, you couldn't run gluten-free dough through these newer machines because there was no elasticity.

As I mentioned, the equipment Venice Bakery had been using for years to make regular wheat-based pizza required more labor than these faster state-of-the-art machines. Fortuitously, however, we actually had a competitive advantage with our equipment when we went down the gluten-free path. We had equipment that was, granted, *old*…but could process and manufacture a tremendous product nobody else wanted to invest in because it was such a new category. The Nestlés and the Schwan's of the world weren't going to spend tens of millions of dollars on additional equipment to go into an unproven category. The risk for them was significant. It was a lot less risky to come to us, a proven co-packer, and say, "Hey, can you make this for us?"

Our value-add to existing brands was clear. We had intellectual property (IP) nobody else had. And we were protective of it; we didn't allow any visitors in the factory to see what equipment we were using or our process. We actually put up curtains in the facility around the production line for when we did walkthroughs with some of our customers (who could have ultimately become one of our competitors).

Our manufacturing equipment and line in El Segundo, CA.

Our process may have been slow but perfect for the consistency of this new batter-like texture of a dough. For all seven years during our company's growth, we kept using this original, slower equipment, but it was not enough to keep pace with projected growth. As we looked to expand and set up a second line, we searched all over the country, including equipment manufacturers, auctions, and even foreclosed manufacturing plants. Fortunately, Jimmy was made aware of a full production line at a foreclosed bakery 3,000 miles away on the East Coast. Jimmy recalls spending a total of $20,000 at that auction, which also included the oven, proofer, and two spiral coolers. Not having a full engineering team working for us, we hired the mechanics from the foreclosed bakery to come out to California and put the line together.

We then needed to obtain a mixer, a dough divider, cooling conveyors, and our proprietary equipment. We again bought much of the line at auctions and then reached out to some of the well-known manufacturers for other equipment.

"In fact," Jimmy said recently, "The company that was making some of the equipment we were using was about to go out of business. I called them and said, 'Do not shut your doors. I think I may have found a new life for your equipment.' And they're still around today. I think our product actually saved their business because nobody was buying older processing equipment anymore until we came back calling. It was too labor-intensive. But that's what we needed."

In business, some equipment that may seem outdated or obsolete to one company can be a valuable asset to another. By recognizing this, you can uncover hidden value and gain a competitive edge.

Premium Price Point

One of the biggest obstacles we faced in those early days after I arrived was trying to sell new customers on the high price of our product. Not only were we introducing a brand-new product in a new category that was considered either a fad or a trend, but we were tasked with selling this product at a premium.

Nobody wanted to give us serious consideration without quite a bit of pushback. I had no data on sales of gluten-free pizza. Zero. The only data I had in my research was the percentage of the population of celiac and gluten-intolerant individuals. At that time, about one percent of the population was diagnosed with celiac disease, and six percent of the population had a gluten intolerance. Having the research to support us (and showing the growing celiac and gluten-intolerant population) was staggering and hard to dismiss. However, it was still not an easy task because that percentage represented a small fraction of the overall pizza market.

Although the percentage was low, it actually translated to a big number because demand didn't stop there. The growing number of celiac and gluten-intolerant populations had an impact on everyone making the decision of where to eat. We liked to use a dartboard as an analogy.

The gluten-free market, including the celiac population and the gluten-intolerant population, is represented on your dartboard. Everybody tries to hit that bull's-eye, which we identify as the celiac population: too small and difficult to target. Next, the inner ring is the gluten-intolerant population: not as small as the celiac population and much more achievable to reach. The rest of the dartboard is the population eating pizza with zero issues.

I'll explain it here just like I explained it to potential Venice Bakery accounts back in 2011: If a group of four people were going out to a pizzeria, as an example, the person who had the allergies made the decision about where to eat. So, if you did not have a gluten-free pizza on your menu, you could be potentially losing that *entire group* of diners. In other words, you want to satisfy the people making decisions—the inner part of the dartboard.

This analysis worked well, but we weren't an overnight success. It took a little while until the products were positioned in the distributors' facilities, in cold storage throughout the country. Once we achieved that, it was much easier for a customer to order directly with their distributors in any amount they needed.

The Master Distributor

With our footprint we were ahead of the game, especially after we were able to get our product moving through an organization called Dot Foods. It's one of the largest food service redistribution companies in the United States, offering over 125,000 products from thousands of food industry manufacturers. Our national distribution through Dot Foods played a key role in helping Venice Bakery expand so quickly.

Here's how it worked. Prior to our relationship with Dot and the ability to offer products nationally at an affordable price, we would be packaging and shipping pallets and sometimes cases of pizza crusts to a specific distributor wherever that customer was throughout the United States. The freight footprint was very expensive, and we faced the inconvenience of creating one single invoice per distributor. This was a logistical nightmare because you can imagine all the different distributors across the country.

Dot Foods, however, allowed us to use their process as a master redistributor. They would pick up products from Venice Bakery and move them to one of their twelve different national distribution centers in key locations across the country. The relationship with them allowed us to bill one distributor, Dot Foods. Now, getting into Dot was not an easy task. They required manufacturers like us to meet certain production capacities, which at the time was about 400,000 pounds per year!

Dot would then take the orders from their customers—the large and independent food distributors around the country—place the order with us, pick up the much larger quantities of orders than we were receiving from the distributors themselves, store them in their frozen warehouses, and then redistribute the cases of pizza crusts to the distributors who would service their end users. This process of redistribution was a win-win for all parties.

Imagine the workload Dot Foods eliminated for us! It alleviated a huge amount of paperwork as well. Instead of creating invoices for all these independent food service distributors (who at times wanted to short-pay their invoices), we didn't have to do that anymore. Instead, our invoices were to Dot directly.

As I mentioned, getting into Dot Foods was a process; there was work to do before Dot would even consider taking us on. We had to grind it out for a little while to get there.

I saw that Dot Foods was where we were headed and it was clearly the most efficient way for us to grow even faster.

15

Tasting The Unexpected

Introducing an unknown, unproven product into an established food category was not easy. It took lots of planning, dedication, and strategic alliances. How did we get people to take us seriously and see the same vision we did? We had to overcome the fact that gluten-free products had a reputation for tasting pretty bad. (You can find some really unappealing stuff even today, in fact.) This made people reluctant to give us a shot.

Our most successful—and really, our only—form of marketing was our presence at trade shows. The trade shows we attended each year included the International Pizza Expo in Las Vegas, the National Restaurant Show in Chicago, and the Private Label show that rotated cities annually. They required lots of planning and preparation. We reserved our booth space each year, and had our booth delivered and set up for each show. We secured staffing, reserved rooms, and had products shipped and held in frozen storage.

We made the shows as fun as possible, engaging with all of the passersby. By turning these long, tiring days into a fun event, we wanted people to leave there with a memorable and lasting impression of our company. We were real people who cared about all of our customers.

We got a lot of people stopping at our booths. Then, they gave us the time of the day because they tasted the unexpected. Watching the expressions on people's faces as they ate was extremely rewarding. The most common feedback and question we got was, "Are you *sure* this is gluten-free?"

In fact, this question became such a predictable one that we had branded T-shirts made, printing this question on the front. The back featured a large "Yes!" along with the Venice Bakery logo.

Our staff wore these shirts and generously gave them out at all of our trade shows. The pleasure we saw on our customers' faces and the acceptance of our vision was starting to show.

In the early days, we designed and created our own trade show booth. Each year, we built it and set it up in our factory, took it down, put it on our small cube truck, and drove it to Las Vegas (as an example), where the International Pizza Expo was held. There, we unpacked everything and set it up, and then we had three days standing on our feet, a minimum of eight hours per day. In addition, we were also going to dinner with potential customers or existing ones, and back at it at eight o'clock the next morning. Finally, we broke down our booth three days later, the same way we started. After a couple of years of this grinding routine, we hired a top trade show booth company out of Florida called GAI Exhibits to handle all of the booth logistics.

At that time, we had two salespeople. Roman Gonzalez had experience working for Sysco Food Distribution and provided a lot of insight into the distributor mindset. Roman did a great job for us thanks to his contacts with distributors and end users like restaurant owners and retail outlets. The other person on our team was Shannon Pritchett, who came to us from Farmer John's. She also had good experience working with the end user and was able to utilize her network and pitch them on this new gluten-free pizza crust.

The quality of our product was the fuel to our success and one of the biggest differentiators when compared to our competition. The question was, "How do we capture more of this market?"

In addition to our food shows, our sales team would conduct a lot of cuttings, a side-by-side test to compare other gluten-free pizza crusts available. Fortunately, almost invariably, restaurants preferred our crusts over the competition. For the most part, our crusts were sold directly to the end user through local distribution. Using our formula, known as "white-labeling", made up the bulk of our business model.

We consistently took our customer's feedback seriously; we were always willing to adjust our recipes, even create custom formulations and sizing when we could. This is commonly known as "private labeling," which I define more in the next section. Again, it was about building trust and a feeling of collaboration so the customer would feel completely comfortable moving forward with us as their partner and pizza crust supplier. I'd learned a lot since my days in my previous start-ups and knew that relationship-building was everything. As I mentioned previously, a personal relationship is just as important as a business relationship. This helps build trust, loyalty, and a deeper connection that can lead to long-term success.

Private Label and White Label

In the beginning, we said yes to almost all customer requests. We were both a White Label company and a Private Label company. Let me define "white label" here: we had an existing formulation that was proprietary to us and sold under the Venice Bakery brand in food service.

We were also a "private label" product manufacturer, which meant that the customer would come to us and ask us to tweak our formulation to meet their specific requirements, needs, or wants, and then sell the product under their own name.

The trade shows were where we did most of our marketing and received the best bang for our buck. We got our products out to a large group of decision-makers in a very short time at these events, and the feedback from the trade show buyers was overwhelmingly positive.

As I have mentioned several times as it is worth repeating, even with all of the positive trends behind us, including the first-to-market benefit and having the highest-quality and best-tasting "on-trend" product, at times it was difficult to get everyone to buy into this entirely new category. The biggest objection we regularly faced was: "Why do I want this? The market's too small."

We explained our dartboard analogy to them, and our pitch started to resonate more and more as time went on. We also benefited a *lot* from being first-to-market. If we were trying to break into gluten-free pizza today, we'd be faced with stiff competition. Being first-to-market with a new product is often seen as a significant advantage for several reasons: being a market leader; establishing customer loyalty; setting industry standards and controlling market share. We benefited from all of these advantages.

Things were looking great.

* * *

I came out to California in October of 2010, Columbus Day weekend. The plan, as I wrote earlier, was to give it a year. During that initial time period, I lived in the basement of Jimmy's house before finding a studio apartment down the street, three miles from the El Segundo facility. I drove a little Prius that Jimmy had as an extra car. I didn't have an office; I was just working on his side desk…putting in long hours, learning the business.

I didn't really know anybody in California other than Jimmy and his family. I was not going out partying or looking for anything to do besides work. My mind was completely wrapped around Venice, all day, every day. I was fully invested in making this company as successful as it could be, because there wasn't anything at this point in my life to fall back on. I was in my mid-forties by then; the thought of this not working and starting over again never crossed my mind. Considering the medical setbacks I'd experienced and the financial situation I was in, this was it for me. I didn't know what else to do if Venice Bakery did not succeed. I was extremely grateful for this opportunity from Jimmy. I was not going to let him or anyone down. Looking back on it, I may have put a lot of pressure on myself. Thankfully, it was worth it.

The plan was clear: I was going to give it 110% and make *sure* it worked. The stakes were high, and so were the rewards if this business was successful. This was the opportunity I had been looking for, and I knew that if I gave it my all, I would not have any regrets even if things didn't work out. This is an important point as it provides some nuance to the message that it is okay to fail. While this is true, there comes a time in life when failure has bigger consequences, especially when you have people depending on you. Failure at a younger age when you are single, for example, is a different thing than failure when you are older and people are relying on your efforts. Our risk tolerance decreases as we get older. When I came home in the evenings after dinner at Jimmy's house with his family, or out for a bite by myself, I'd do pretty much one thing: think about the company—"How do we make this successful? What do we need to do next? Where do I see this company in three years? Five years?"

In order to keep our ducks in a row and be sure we were following a plan that could be sustainable, I wrote a business plan in my spare time. I remember our CPA said it was one of the best business plans he'd ever read, and at that moment, I felt very confident that we were on a path to success. The focus I had during those seven years is an important factor contributing to the major growth of the company.

As of this writing, my daughter Audrey had recently learned how to ride a bike. She was determined to learn and take the training wheels off. She fought hard, was so determined, and was getting confident and proud of herself, so I said to her, "Are you ready? *I* know you are. Once these training wheels come off, they don't go back on." Her determination paid off! I like this as an analogy. Once you go all in, you're not coming back out. And that's when the magic happens.

I've heard this over and over from successful people and peers: "I went all in—financially, emotionally, mentally. You've got to give it your all. If you don't give 110%, odds are that it may not work."

My dad always told me that it doesn't matter what you do, as long as you do your best. Find something that you love to do and do it better than anyone else, and give it your all.

* * *

Focusing on food service such as restaurants and pizzerias, we initially accepted orders as small as a few cases and sent them out via FedEx on dry ice! As you can imagine, this was extremely expensive and inefficient for the end user. In an effort to drive down costs, we needed to sell to more accounts. This would allow distributors to step in, helping us to meet the growing demand and lower costs for our customers. A local distributor would take a more moderately-sized order because it was logistically feasible for them, but a national distributor needed pallet-sized orders or more.

Over time, we escalated production to orders of as much as one pallet (approximately 150 cases). This was the result of our marketing efforts at the trade shows and end users requesting their distributors to carry our brand of crusts. Then came private label requests from national food brands and national grocery store chains. As mentioned, each trade show has a different audience.

After Domino's launched gluten-free pizza in 2012, the market started to pay attention. As the market became aware of this trend, Venice was positioned to capitalize due to our high-quality products and position in the marketplace.

16

I Do

When interviewing Carla for my salon back in 2003, there was definitely an immediate attraction. I was single then… going out, having fun with my friends, and traveling. She wasn't much of a partier and didn't care about going out much; instead, she had always been a hard worker. Carla took care of her mother, and she put her clients first. As our potential relationship was building, we started spending more time together.

I remember our first date. I asked her to meet me at my favorite restaurant, Al Forno in Providence, Rhode Island. (To this day, it's our favorite restaurant in the state and probably in my top five in the country.) We sat at the bar—a comfortable and casual way to chat—and it was great. I remember learning more and more about her life, how hard she had to work, and the different jobs she juggled to pay the mortgage, car payment, and all other obligations.

One night when we were having dinner at a restaurant where her friend was working, I remember telling her, "I think it's time someone starts taking care of *you*."

Those words hit home. For some reason, and fortunately, she believed in me.

I explained that sometimes, even though you're strong, you need to have some vulnerability, to take a risk. She was hesitant. I said, "You need to let your guard down in order to experience what may be a good thing."

And she did.

From that point we started dating, and not long afterward, I suffered seizures and surgery for my brain tumor. I was in the hospital and, of course, Carla was regularly visiting me.

My sister always said, "You're going to marry her." I answered, "No, I'm never getting married again." (I was briefly married earlier in life.)

But sure enough, Carla had started getting familiar with my family, and our relationship was really developing. As I was recovering from my brain tumor, I was getting back to work and listening to my doctor's orders more seriously at this time and, thus, did not engage in a lot of partying. When I made the decision to come to California, she supported me; she never said no. After we agreed that California and Venice Bakery was best for me, we planned for her to permanently relocate and come out west in January of 2012. However, she said she wasn't going to move unless she knew our relationship was going somewhere even further.

We had plans to go to Italy with three other couples in 2011. We all rented a villa together. First, I flew back to Boston and spent a couple of days there with Carla and my family. From there, Carla and I flew to Lake Como for three days. I had reached out to a friend of mine, Michael Petrarca, for the best place to stay, and he recommended Grand Hotel Villa Serbelloni. His suggestion as to the best place to stay was on point!

Before we left for our trip, I'd done my homework. My mother was in the jewelry business, and I was familiar with a local custom jeweler in downtown LA as well. I had gotten a ring made and my intent, obviously, was to get engaged at Lake Como.

Villa Serbelloni overlooked Lake Como, and across the lake were the mountains of Switzerland...pretty amazing. The food was terrific. The coffee was incredible. I mean, I never drank so much coffee in my life. Toward the end of dinner on our last night there, I got down on one knee, and Carla said yes. We started calling family and friends back home.

* * *

The next day, we drove to Tuscany to meet our friends. During the trip, we stopped at a small pizzeria in the hills where the exporter of flour and other products to Whole Foods had invited us to meet him. Because we did so much work with Whole Foods Market, he had said, "Listen, when you get to Italy, contact me. I want to show you around."

Once there, they treated us like royalty. They took me to the back and showed me the ovens they used and the dough, which they made each day. Everything, of course, was done by hand. Eating there was such an amazing experience. When it was time to go, I asked, "Here's where I'm going in Tuscany. Can you please tell me how to get to the villa where we are staying?"

I was driving a larger Mercedes on the tiny rural Italian roads, simply because the car rental agency was out of the smaller vehicles when we arrived (the roads in Italy are very narrow, so most cars are generally small). We punched the directions that we had gotten into the car's GPS, and for some reason, instead of taking us around the side of the hill that the villa was on, his directions took us more or less *over* it. It was starting to get dark, and we were *lost*. We got up towards the peak of the mountain and looked for any help we could find. Nobody was around. Finally, I saw a structure. I pulled over, and there were a bunch of extremely friendly Italian folks hanging around, as well as a bunch of animals, including chickens, goats, etc. I got out of the car and asked, "Can you help me with this?" Nobody spoke English. They started drawing in the sand with a stick, but it was obvious this was not going to work. I had no idea what to do!

Finally, one gentleman jumped in his pickup truck and gestured to follow him. I had no choice but to do so, even though I didn't know where he was taking us. But what was I going to do? I trusted him, and he got us to the villa and my friends in ten minutes! I tried to pay him for his time, but he would not take a dime. His generosity was truly from his heart.

The next day, we all made arrangements to go for a scenic ride. While I was driving, I had a seizure, went off the side of the road, flipped the car over, and woke up to medical personnel pulling me out of the car. Fortunately, no one else got hurt; everyone was fine. But the next thing I knew, I was in the hospital in Italy.

I stayed there overnight for tests. While the doctors did not find anything earth-shattering, Carla was not surprised by this based on her experience of seeing me go through seizures in the past. I was discharged twenty-four hours later. The next day, we spent some time in Tuscany, drove through Siena, and stopped for lunch while making our way to Florence before heading back home a few days later. Upon our return, Carla and I started planning our wedding, which was on August 11, 2013. It was down in Dana Point in California at the Ritz-Carlton, a destination wedding for our guests from Rhode Island. For our honeymoon, we chose Bora Bora. A dream beginning to our life together, to say the least.

17

The Hockey Stick

As our product proved itself in Whole Foods Market stores, they let us grow to more regions, and eventually, we achieved a national distribution level with them. We started with Southern California, expanded to Northern California and the Southwest. As sales within the company kept growing, Whole Foods kept expanding our reach across the country. Another major account we landed at the same time was Sprouts Farmers Market, a national grocery chain in over thirty states. Similar to the Whole Foods movement, we started in the Southern Californian region and continued to expand East. We were now seeing revenues grow in both food service and grocery.

But the real big one, the one that put us on the map and how many of our would-be customers came to find out about us, was Domino's in 2012.

The meeting with Domino's happened thanks to a former employee of theirs who was then independently acting as a sales rep for new products. Domino's wasn't happy with what he was showing them as a gluten-free option, so he was on the search for an alternative one.

Through several rounds of samplings, quality assurances, and factory visits, they agreed to give us a chance. Since this was an unproven market, it was obviously a risk and an opportunity for them.

There was no slow rollout like there had been with many of our previous customers. Domino's ordered *truckloads* of product at a time, equivalent to over 60,000 pizza crusts! However, they kept their marketing for the new offering minimal, to say the least. In fact, we kept saying they could've blown this thing out of the water if they put some marketing behind it—like they did with everything else. Perhaps for them, offering gluten-free pizza but not marketing it was a trial period situation. We didn't know. But for us, regardless, it was a big deal to get that account.

* * *

The Domino's account forced production time in the El Segundo facility to immediately increase. Jimmy and I thought, *Okay, we're doing X number of dollars now in this building. If the business continues to grow like this, the only way forward is to get another building.* This was a crucial time for me to analyze and forecast our business to ensure sustained growth for long-term success. I was looking at our opportunities, and tracking industry trends and potential challenges we could face. This proactive approach helped us make informed decisions and mitigate risks. The decision to expand production was easy.

The property we found in Torrance, California, fourteen miles from our original facility, was much bigger than what we needed. In fact, 60,000 sq. ft. compared to 11,000 sq. ft. The thing we loved about the new facility was that, compared to other buildings we were looking at, there were no columns in the middle of the space, a wide open floor plan, allowing for straight production lines. This particular building was very well designed by Henry Weber, a seasoned German individual with great foresight. The El Segundo facility, by comparison, was not an efficient setup, though we used every single square foot of it and maxed out its capabilities.

The biggest obstacle at that point was the price of the new building: *How would we afford a multi million building?* It was the largest capital investment decision we had faced up to that point. The real estate market favored buyers in 2012, and we knew we had the upper hand in our negotiations. Fortunately for us, the building had been vacant for almost two years, so Jimmy was able to secure a good price. While real estate acquisition can be an obstacle for other businesses due to overall market conditions, it presented a real opportunity for us at that time. The price we negotiated was below the value the bank had placed on it, and thus, we were able to obtain a loan with favorable terms. It was a big risk but ultimately worthwhile.

"I'll never forget when I walked my father into that 60,000-square-foot building we had bought," Jimmy said recently. "He stood there, looked around, and said, 'Are you sure you want all this stress?' Today, this building is probably putting out 300,000 pizza crusts a day.

"It all goes back to your risk-tolerance level," Jimmy continued. "When you're older, you don't have any risk tolerance. But when you're young, you have all the risk tolerance in the world. In our case, it was like we were playing poker. We had two aces in the hole, and we had no choice but to push all the chips on the table. Which is exactly what we did, time after time after time. We had favorable circumstances working for us. The real estate market couldn't have been better—there was no better time to buy and invest in a building than in 2012. Interest rates were beginning to fall; the business was growing leaps and bounds. Our quarterly reports to the bankers allowed us to get cheap money, all we needed whenever we needed it, to help us continue to grow the business."

At the time, Jimmy and I looked at each other and said, "We better find a way to fill it up!"

After the purchase of the Torrance facility, the first thing we needed was to install a new manufacturing line.

We had limited capital due to the real estate purchase, so that's when we purchased equipment from foreclosed East Coast bakeries. (Never underestimate the value of being resourceful and creative when you run a business.) This was a crucial point for us. We were faced with the decision to consider taking in some outside funding, which was available to us due to the success and trajectory of the business to date, or to bootstrap the business ourselves. Any time an entrepreneur takes on outside financing, usually in exchange for equity, they are immediately on the clock. Investors are looking to get a return on their money within a period of time (usually three to five years), so they will be monitoring growth very closely. Instead, Jimmy and I decided to reject all outside investment inquiries. We wanted to focus on our customers' needs, get to know our market more, and stay focused on what we do best. We did not want to be distracted by investor needs or requirements. I often get asked for the single best bit of advice that I would give any entrepreneur, and it's this: If you can bootstrap your own venture as long as possible, do it.

In Torrance, we had the ability to run our manufacturing in a straight line, due to the forward-thinking building layout. This was, in fact, one of the most attractive characteristics of the building in the decision to purchase it in 2012. We installed some insulated walls down the middle to minimize cross-contamination in the plant, which allowed us to continue manufacturing both wheat-based products initially and gluten-free products at the same time. (On the wheat-based side, we were making dough balls, but by 2017 we eliminated our wheat-based production completely.) We required our employees to enter the building from the back entrance, and if they were working on gluten-free production, they'd come in on one side; if they were working on wheat-based production, they'd come in on the other side of the building. We even had separate production team locker rooms upstairs, as we were taking all steps necessary to eliminate any cross-contamination.

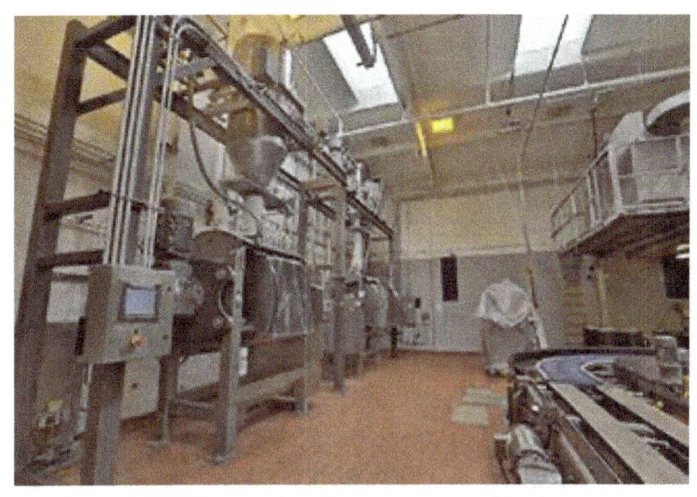

Pictured: Our spacious new Torrance facility.

* * *

Our fast growth at Venice Bakery did not come without its hiccups. At first, not having a full-time, experienced maintenance and engineering team on staff caused many logistical issues. We did have mechanics on staff, and they were able to handle the day-to-day issues that arose. Yet, when a line or a piece of critical equipment went down, we had to call in additional outside contractors to help with repairs.

At one point fairly early in my role, I hired a production manager who was referred to us and came with industry experience. However, because this gluten-free pizza manufacturing process was a completely new category, the learning curve was a bit longer than we anticipated for him, and had to start a new search for a person who had experience with allergen- free food products. These personnel challenges are common when anyone is entering into a new space. Quite naturally, there was not enough history for anyone to fill a production role with significant experience because of the category's infancy.

Everybody said our growth resembled a hockey stick. There were also spikes and then quieter times when we were preparing for the next spike. That's when we had to do a lot of work to get ready. Did we always make the right decisions? Not all the time. Sometimes we rushed into hiring. Things worked for a little while, but we knew our employees weren't happy with the instability, so we made a conscious effort to be more diligent in our hiring process moving forward.

I believe the best practice is to hire based on character and someone's willingness to work. There are always opportunities to train and coach an individual on the business and the position that they are hired for, as long as they have the qualities that are hard to teach: character and passion. If they have that passion and want to work and have good character, that individual will succeed much faster than the person with a ton of knowledge but less willingness to work. One bad seed can ruin the apple.

* * *

After purchasing the Torrance building in 2012, Jimmy and I flew to Germany to attend the largest bakery equipment show in the world. The IBA Trade Fair hosted over 1,300 exhibitors and 77,000 visitors from over 160 countries. We knew that if we were to continue to grow and expand our business at the rate we were going, we needed to find more efficient ways to do so. Our goal, then, was to go out and find a way to convert the art of gluten-free crust-making into a *science*. Keep in mind that our first two production lines required lots of manual labor and were not automated. No updated technology was involved, so human error was an ongoing concern.

Therefore, the first way we could immediately expand was to figure out how to add production while not adding to our biggest cost, labor. We sought automated equipment that would afford us this goal—and we knew that if there was any place in the world we would find this equipment, it was at this show in Germany. It was all about reducing human error and making our product more standardized.

Sure enough, we were able to find automated mixing equipment, automated proofing equipment, automated packaging equipment, and more. Jimmy and I chatted for quite some time on the plane trip home. We talked about the equipment that we saw and how we could apply it to the growth of the company, how we could scale production, what our biggest opportunities were, what main risks we faced, and what contingencies we would need to have in place in case of any setbacks, among many other business-related items. The manufacturing footprint of the building in Torrance, all 45,000 square feet of it, was not yet at capacity. However, it was becoming quite clear what equipment we needed to make full use of the space.

I love technology and relish getting ahead of the game by leveraging it. When I saw the automated dispensing systems, for example, I knew they were the way forward despite the steep price tag. If we were going to grow the way that we wanted to and the way that the market demanded, we had to take the risk of buying more advanced equipment. After I calculated the return on our investment, Jimmy and I decided to bet on ourselves and take this risk. This was an intimidating decision. Jimmy had just purchased a $5 million building, so contemplating spending even more wasn't easy.

In my opinion, however, that newer equipment was not simply an option; it was a necessity. It would allow us to keep moving forward. The trip to Germany was not only a successful one from a strategic operations perspective, but also one that organically developed into an equity ownership discussion, a true business partnership instead of a friends/employer/employee relationship. I felt that my hard work and dedication were recognized and rewarded as a result. We came up with an agreement that day! At that time, neither Jimmy nor I intended to sell the family business. To be honest, I didn't have equity on my mind when we started the conversation. That part of the discussion organically developed while we were chatting. My thinking and transparency evolved into, "If I'm going to do all this work, moving away from my family and friends, giving my 100% helping grow this business, it has to make sense for me in the long run." Jimmy agreed.

Jimmy owned 100% of Venice Bakery because he had previously bought out his brother, and he's always been fair. He's probably one of the most fair and reasonable individuals I know to this day. Thus, it was only right that we talked about me having some equity in the business at that point.

18

Branding & Certifications

Sprouts Farmers Market encouraged us to create a Venice Bakery-branded product for their shelves. We were resistant to partnering with Sprouts to do this as it would have been a completely different business model for us to launch our own brand...and it would have been extremely expensive and challenging.

The positive side of creating and marketing your own branded product is that your brand is recognizable and potentially more valuable. We never had a brand in the marketplace. Instead, we preferred our private label and white label model. As the customer, you didn't know Venice Bakery, you just knew the store brand 365, for instance, and you assumed Whole Foods made that food item—a fair assumption.

There was a time when you could walk into a super-market and see many different branded frozen gluten-free pizzas—and we probably had about a 60% share of that market. Six of every ten brands of gluten- free pizza were using our crusts! Therefore, if we had decided to take our pizza, brand it, and put it next to another pizza brand (which we were most likely making for someone else), we would have lost a lot of credibility and sales because we would have been competing with our own customers. This was not a fair thing to do to them. If we had decided to change our business model and take that approach, the companies and stores we were making pizza crusts for may have sourced their product from a company not competing with them.

As much as there's a benefit to having your own brand, in our case, we felt it was more beneficial for us not to. We didn't care what name was on the product, as long as we were getting it to the end user...pizza lovers!

* * *

Sprouts Farmers Market was not the only store to come to us and ask for a Venice Bakery branded gluten-free pizza. These situations were difficult for us, to say the least. We were already private labeling for our customers who had relationships with these grocery stores. When these retailers were selling our customer's branded products and then they came to us to sell a private label product under the store's own brand, we had to toe a delicate line. Did we want to say no to the retailer and risk them going to a competitor? Or did we want to say yes to the store-branded private label opportunity, yet risk our relationship with our customers?

We ultimately decided that in the best interest of all involved, we would be transparent with our customers so they would have an opportunity to strengthen their relationship with the retailer. Most of the time in these cases, our customers would come to us and ask us to lower our prices to them, knowing that the retailer would get a better price coming to us directly since they did not have to pay any markup that our customer had built in.

In the end, we worked as best as possible to help our customers make their margins work without sacrificing quality.

Certifications

Whole Foods, Trader Joe's, and others used to have what they called a "No-No List." As a supplier, you could not have any of those ingredients in your products. The list included things like preservatives, dyes, and sweeteners that we had never used. We preserved our crusts using a natural mold inhibitor, as well as freezing them. They were also asking for additional certifications, some of which we had, and others that we didn't. But we always wanted to satisfy the customer. *If you need this,* we always said, *you'll have it.*

Obtaining any and all recognizable certifications was a win for all involved. It would satisfy our customers' requests and strengthen the quality of our products. Some were more difficult to get than others, but in the end, it further separated us from the competition.

All of these particular requirements led us to hire our QA department director, Ulises Gonzalez, a talented professional who went on to lead our research and development team as well. Our first QA Director had been Michael Greene. He came to us on the recommendation from our ingredient supplier's representative, Trish Dozier. You'll remember that Trish was influential in introducing Jimmy to the unique raw materials in 2009 that set our gluten-free pizza crusts apart from all others.

Michael had a bit of QA experience; however, as the business started to grow and we were growing as a company, our customers were demanding and requiring more certifications and audits. In 2013, Michael came to us asking for help. He felt that in order to maintain his roles and responsibilities that were required of him in the daily operations and to meet the demands of our growing customer base, we needed to bring in a seasoned QA director to handle the certification part of the business.

This led to the hiring of Ulises. After hiring Ulises, our QA department started to grow organically. We ended up hiring additional staffing to support the entire team, keep detailed records of data, and ensure that all products entering the facility met our specs so we would not be subject to any food recalls.

Our new focus on quality assurance was based on our commitment to quality. When we launched our product with Domino's, their main concern was its gluten-free status. Domino's needed to know we had less than a certain level of parts per million (ppm) when we tested for gluten. As I mentioned, the FDA mandated below twenty parts per million to qualify a product to be gluten-free; we held it to below five ppm. At that time, we were still using the in-house testing kits. We moved on from relying on only in-house test kits once it became clear we needed further certification as the industry was starting to expand. That's when we reached out to third-party certifiers for validations.

19

"Pull Not Push" Philosophy

Venice Bakery products went through big food distributors such as Sysco, US Foods, and many others. Our customers were already sourcing different food products from these distributors as it would be illogical to expect a reasonably priced product to go from one coast to the other coast in a small quantity while being cost-effective. For us to expand nationally, we needed to figure out a way to make it feasible for the distributor to purchase a minimum order and have it be enough for them to pick it up, store the product, *and* move it across the country efficiently. Distributors do not want to sit on product and thus need to move product in and out of their warehouse as quickly as possible (which helps them with their margins).

In the beginning, of course, the question was, "How do we get the product to the distributors?" Relying on distributors to sell your product is not uncommon, but since this gluten-free category was new, and gluten-free pizza was new to the category, distributors were very reluctant to take a chance on the product. Thus, we had a difficult time convincing them to take that chance. Instead, we used what we called a "pull not push" philosophy, meaning that we relied on our end customer requesting our product from their distributor, who would ask something like, "Hey, I want Venice Bakery's gluten-free pizza crust. Can you please find a way to get that for me?"

If we had enough customers doing this, it relieved our burden of trying to push our product through distributors. To get customers to ask for Venice Bakery crusts, we attended trade shows. The idea was to reach customers in person so they would then put pressure on their distributor and request our product. If enough customers asked for our product, then the distributor would come to us and place a reasonably-sized purchase order, which both satisfied our minimum orders and made it worthwhile for the distributor. Although a great strategy, it could potentially take a long time until either the distributor had enough requests to place a reasonable size order or until the distributor believed in the product enough to take a leap of faith and place a minimum order that met both their requirements and ours.

The redistributor Dot Foods (which I introduced earlier in the book) filled these types of issues for distributors. Dot re-distributed truckloads of products from manufacturers to distributors, large and small, around the country. Back then, as long as the distributor was placing an order total of 5,000 pounds with Dot, they could order as little as one case of any product from them! Since Dot Foods had required manufacturers to be producing a minimum of 400,000 pounds of their product for Dot alone, Venice could not work with them until we reached that level in 2014.

* * *

Our work was all about high-quality products, good customer service, and increasing supply. The demand was out there. There were endless nights of strategizing over "How do we continue to grow? How do we expand this business in a quality fashion?" Thankfully, we did not have any quality issues or food-related recalls.

For industry leaders like Schwan's, Nestlé, and even Domino's, the gluten-free category was an unproven market. They were unwilling, nor did it make sense for them, to dedicate a large amount of resources, time, and money to this category. Instead, it was more beneficial for them to use a co-packer like Venice to test the market.

When the market grew beyond a certain point, the bigger players had the resources to change their strategy.

The good news for us was that we had *such* a phenomenal formulation of gluten-free pizza crust in terms of taste and an IP around our process that the barrier to entry to those industry leaders appeared to be significant. Our first-to-market positioning gave us a leg up and put us ahead of everyone—more than we even realized. We were just a small company from El Segundo, California, competing with big companies, including a behemoth out of Buffalo, New York, called Rich Products, a four billion dollar food manufacturer, which you'll read more about soon. However, we later came to find out that they were only doing a million dollars a year in gluten-free pizza. That's relatively insignificant for them. Because we didn't really know those numbers at the time, we thought, "How are *we* going to compete with Rich Products?" Yet our strong results spoke for themselves.

Good Cop/Bad Cop

At the trade shows, Jimmy was the one everyone wanted to see, the one the customers wanted to go out with. I was not going out till three in the morning; that wasn't me. I was in bed by nine. Ha! Jimmy's willingness to wine and dine customers, to connect with them at these events as a true friend, and to go out all night if need be was important to Venice Bakery's trajectory because I believe that you do business with people first, and people wanted to do business with Jimmy. My role was to get the job done behind the scenes; his role was to network and generate sales. A true synergy of our talents working together.

On a regular day, if we got inquiries from local pizzerias or local distributors, we would turn those leads over to our salespeople, Roman or Shannon. If it was a larger customer like Domino's, Papa John's, California Pizza Kitchen, or Blaze Pizza, those would go directly to Jimmy and me. Jimmy would find out more about what they were interested in, as he could talk the talk better than I could when it came to industry jargon and history. We'd then work together on some details on pricing and volume, and then Jimmy would follow up with them to close the sale. I would then take over with operations.

Outside of his very important sales and networking role, Jimmy had a strong presence on the manufacturing floor. He would check on production efficiency, address any equipment issues, and attend to any production-related issues. My focus was different; I had come in with a mission, a big audacious goal in mind. I had the ability to help scale the company in terms of operations and systems, including loss reduction and growth.

Although Jimmy was naturally aggressive and motivated, it would have been a difficult task to scale the business alone. Our pace together was *much* faster. It was also chaotic, growing a valuation of over fifty times in just seven years. We were dealing with anything and everything possible, and no two days were alike. We were hiring people, putting in new lines for equipment, selling new accounts, and dealing with customer service issues nonstop every single day. We had to wear multiple hats at all hours, and we were there every day. And happy to do it!

My job was to maximize the margins and hold the line on our pricing quotes as much as possible. We were a team, and I knew my role was important. I had great detail into every aspect of our business. I knew what our margins had to be. Jimmy knew that he could focus on generating new business. Together, we would be sure to support the growth with expanded infrastructure.

In sports, each player has their position to play. Yet, they all play together as a team and there is a good reason that a team works. Sure, we discussed certain business decisions; however, in the end we always found common ground.

You hear stories of so much success in the business world, and the question is, *how were we different from others?* In our case, it was for all the reasons I've discussed so far, but it was also because besides being good friends and good working partners, Jimmy and I are respectful of each other. We have different skills that complemented each other very well, and we were fortunate to be together during this wild and fast ride.

20

Betting On Ourselves

Intuition will tell the thinking mind
where to look next.
—Jonas Salk

When we were sourcing manufacturers for our second-line equipment in the Torrance facility, we needed to mimic the specific manufacturing processes we had in place for our proprietary gluten-free pizza crusts. This required sourcing equipment from several different manufacturers all over the world. It was up to us to find these individual manufacturers and spec out what we needed for them, *and* figure out how to connect everything more efficiently now that our business was growing and speed needed to play a bigger role.

As you can imagine, the commercial and industrial-sized units we needed required a lot of resources. While we had a great mechanical team, we also needed a certified engineering team. As we scaled production, the new line would require a significant amount of engineering to build these pieces of equipment out to our specs while trying to fit everything into a somewhat limited amount of space. Since a larger, more efficient manufacturing line required the skill set of certified engineers, we outsourced different manufacturers that provided additional engineering resources along with their equipment.

As I mentioned, we found our automated batching and dispensing system company while at the show in Munich. We also met with a company that provided our automated packing and proofing system. But we needed more. Much more.

We then came across a company in Ohio called VTech Engineering, which we thought could offer us the services we required, including an oven that would meet our needs. Unfortunately, they were running into some significant financial hardship at the time that we were obviously not aware of. Halfway through the project of building the oven for us, they could not afford to finish it, let alone install or troubleshoot, leaving us with a production line that was only half done! They were sending us digital updates, but we wanted to see for ourselves—in person—if any progress was really happening. We sent one of our lead mechanics, Stan Bruner, out to Ohio to figure out what was going on.

Stan immediately reported back to us the state of affairs at VTech. The reports were not good; progress simply wasn't there.

As a result, we decided to hire VTech's lead mechanic, who was completely transparent with us and willing to relocate to California to help us finish the line. We negotiated a deal with VTech to end their work and send us what they had completed so we could finish it in-house. They shipped the completed oven pieces in module form.

Together with our in-house mechanical team, Stan and Steffen Langstrup (who came from VTech) were able to finish the oven. Steffen knew the inner workings of VTech equipment, and he convinced us that the quality could equal or surpass the other well-known equipment companies out there. With his input, we sourced local engineers to come in and help finish the oven according to our specs without any manufacturer's support. Financially, we had no choice but to spend whatever it took to finish and install the oven.

Our new line problems were a stumbling block in terms of even faster growth, yet one good thing we got out of this stressful situation was a new (very qualified) employee in Steffen. And, once the line was fully commissioned, it increased our output significantly. Even though we had a lot of roadblocks and hurdles to overcome, we were really excited and saw huge potential. We also added additional pieces of equipment that helped us with our efficiency and volume output. During those tricky bottleneck months, we were able to move forward by working extra hours on our first Torrance line to help supplement any shortfalls we had.

* * *

Even though we had significantly upgraded our production line, we still had to maintain our proprietary process to continue to produce good, quality pizza crusts. However, the one thing we could not do was significantly cut down on labor. Our process required a certain number of employees working on the line, regardless of how automated we wanted to make the process.

We were operating with twenty to twenty-five people on these lines instead of twenty-five to thirty people. A very slight cut in labor, to say the least. Our capacity increased, and we had eliminated a lot of opportunities for human errors on the production line—a satisfying win. As we continued to market ourselves by making the market aware of the need to carry a gluten-free pizza, public awareness of gluten-free products in general was starting to become mainstream. This awareness helped contribute to our growth. As Jimmy and I saw capacity increasing and the need to use all 45,000 square feet of the manufacturing space, we then purchased a 30,000-square-foot warehouse directly across the street to help with raw material and equipment storage.

Now that people were becoming familiar with the market demand, celiac disease, and Venice Bakery, I wanted to be sure any and all accreditations for our product were achieved and maintained. In addition to maintaining important certifications on an annual basis, many of our larger customers like Domino's, Papa John's, Nestlé, and Schwan's, to name a few, required their own Quality Assurance teams to come and audit our facility at least annually. Our QA team handled these audits without fail.

21

Trends In Food

From the beginning, Jimmy had a good feeling about helping the families with children who had Autism Spectrum Disorder after getting solid feedback from Dr. Hirani as well as the consumers themselves. Within just a few years, everyone knew Venice Bakery as *the* gluten-free pizza company. And then, the next big wave in the food industry arrived: plant-based foods.

In late 2014 and early 2015, after doing our research, we learned the number-one selling product of Trader Joe's was cauliflower rice. With this data and more, we felt it would be a natural extension of our offerings to add at least a cauliflower gluten-free pizza crust to our product line.

The logical question would be, *well, how did you know how much cauliflower to use, and how did you develop a formula or recipe for this?* It was truly trial and error. We had initially started building the plant-based pizza crust products using cauliflower rice, broccoli, beets, and sweet potatoes. We were making pizza crusts from any kind of vegetable we could, but cauliflower was the ingredient that smashed it out of the park. Our R&D department started to come up with different formulations, and we did focus groups on the new products with our internal staff and an extended group of family and friends. Once we hit upon the best recipe, we were able to scale it up quickly, making thousands of pounds at a time. Since it was also vegan and gluten-free, we did not have to change any disclosures on our labels.

As most parents know, if you try to put a food with any green tint in front of a kid, he or she will take three steps backwards. Our new cauliflower offering luckily had a neutral color and a neutral taste. When a parent would make that pizza for their child and see the plate clear, they'd feel good, especially when the kid started saying, "Hey, Mom, can I have another one of those?" It's pretty gratifying for parents to know that they have put a bunch of vegetables and nutrition in their child's diet.

It was the same thing with the gluten-free product back in the day. The emails we received were so nice—truly heartfelt emails—especially from parents saying, "Oh my gosh, my son ate this whole pizza. Usually, it's one or two bites and he pushes it away. Thanks to you, I looked over and the whole thing was gone."

At the next trade show, we made sure we had a giant banner saying, "Plant-based pizza." Our thinking was clear: *Everybody knows us as a gluten-free pizza company. Now everyone's going to know us as a plant-based pizza company.*

This plant-based crust became a significant part of our business. We were one of the first companies to bring cauliflower pizza crust to market. One other company was out there creating a brand in the space, but they were only in the early stages of bringing retail awareness to the product. We were far ahead, filling the demand of all the private label and white label brands trying to capitalize on this category growth already. It quickly became a high-demand product and contributed to a large percentage of our growth right out of the gate.

* * *

Our gluten-free pizza crust was not intended to be this hugely successful commercial product initially. Instead, it organically grew as a category, thanks to consumer demand for it. We could honestly say to restaurants, "Why would you *not* want to have this at least available? Pizza is a $42 billion industry. You're not going to sell $42 billion in gluten-free items, but you may help increase your sales just by offering it."

We would regularly get pushback from retailers believing that gluten-free was a fad. But a fad is different from a trend, we would explain. A trend is long-lasting, while a fad comes and goes. Gluten-free food wasn't just a fad. It is a trend with strong and growing demand even today. This is due to many reasons, including public awareness and better advancement in medical data leading to more accurate diagnosis, as well as the desire to lead a gluten-free lifestyle. With an Italian background myself, I regularly ate pasta and bread...and I have a sweet tooth. But over the last three years, I've become very health conscious and now understand the benefits of eating right, sleeping, and exercising for longevity and health. I have also cut gluten out of my diet. Luckily for me, you can't go to a place now and *not* find gluten-free options.

As I grew older and became more in tune with my own body, I started investing more in my health. From exercising and eating right, I continue to research the latest food trends, exercise benefits, and self-healing strategies. I've taken up a plant-based diet, I practice yoga and Pilates, and I work out five times per week. Additionally, I meditate on a regular basis, walk regularly, and find myself in a much better place in life than I did as an entrepreneur who was working sixty-plus hours per week.

I like to say that we age from the inside out, and the major things that cause ill feelings and inflammation result from certain foods. For me personally, I have stopped eating gluten and feel better than ever. I know that there are many others out there like myself, and as a result, I believe the growth in this category will continue. In fact, Jimmy and I have discussed the opportunity to put this product in home freezers via a direct-to-consumer sales model.

* * *

Thinking like an entrepreneur, I dedicated many hours to help the business succeed: getting up at 5:30 in the morning, having my coffee and breakfast, and arriving at the factory no later than 6:30. On gym days, I'd wake up at 4:30 a.m., make notes, journal, and have breakfast. I'd leave home at 5:40 to make sure I was at the gym for my training session at 6:00, leave there at 7:00, and be in the office by 7:30 at the latest. Entrepreneurship is not for the faint of heart. It's long hours, uncertainty, and plenty of times that you wonder if it's all worth it.

I always felt that meetings on Thursdays accomplished the most. It gave everybody time on Friday to get ready for the week ahead after thinking about what we talked about and to focus on implementing strategies for the next week.

When you know hard work is par for the course and comes with the territory, it doesn't feel like too much. The first fourteen months after I joined Jimmy and Venice Bakery in California, I was alone. There was nothing else I had to do but work. Things grew more demanding when Jimmy was going through his divorce and the loss of his brother. But I did not see that responsibility as bothersome. I didn't look at it any way other than, "Okay, this is what I need to do." I knew I could be there for him and run the business.

Of course, when you are busy, there are always reasons, or excuses, not to exercise or eat healthy. It's easy to fall out of a healthy lifestyle. It's important to keep an eye on these things if you can. Even though I played lots of sports growing up and stayed active through college, healthy eating was not the easiest, considering where I came from. Back in the seventies and eighties, many plant-based healthy options were not easy to find. In college, healthy eating was not the most affordable option, either. I'm glad things have changed and that Venice Bakery played a small part in the movement.

22

All In On Trade Shows

Since we were determined to keep growing, we had to find new customers while increasing business with our existing ones. We wanted to control our own destiny, so we took a different approach and stuck with it. We kept targeting the end purchasers: restaurants, pizzerias, supermarkets, and private-label brands. Since we were still a small company with only two salespeople at the time, the most efficient way to do so (and reach as many customers as we could, as quickly as we could) was always at trade shows. These trade shows are where all the buyers for the customers we identified would regularly source new products. Some of the shows included the International Pizza Expo, the Private Label Trade Show, the Natural Food Expo, and the National Restaurant Association Show.

When we hung our sign with our tagline: "The Best-Tasting Gluten-Free Pizza," it attracted a lot of people to our booth.

Imagine you're a restaurant buyer for a pizzeria or a buyer for a private label brand walking in from across the hall. You see our sign, and you think, "Okay, I'll try that. Why not?"

It was enticing.

Photo credit: Custom Fabrication & Rental Trade Show Exhibits - G.A.I. Exhibits Project Gallery (gaiexhibits.com)

After the first couple of years of handling the logistics of the trade shows and the booth ourselves, we were in a better position to hire a freight company to pack up a portable oven, our pizzas, our toppings, and all the necessary accessories we needed. During the first few years, we placed online ads to hire brand ambassadors to help cook and serve pizza in every city we were in. Along with our team, which consisted of Jimmy, me, our two salespeople, and other key personnel, we worked ten-hour days cooking, serving, and interacting with key buyers. As needed, Jimmy and I also entertained customers and/or potential customers after the shows and into the night. As we grew, we eventually needed a larger team of ambassadors to help at the booth, so we hired local talent agencies for this.

> We had a ball at those trade shows. We were always winning awards for innovation. One of the things I loved the most was that our competitors would come by and just be like, "Geez, look at these guys. They have a line around their booth."

> That was the greatest thing. And we always knew, every time we went to those shows, that we had to bring in something special. Something different. Once we had money and an R&D team, we were instructing them on what we wanted and getting great results. For example, when we developed a new plant-based recipe using cauliflower, we knew we were going to set the world on fire. It was new. It was on-trend. And it was great tasting. Nobody else had that then.

> The shows were fun, spending quality time with the team and going out to dinners with the team, the vendors, and the customers, continuing to solidify

relationships. Our goal was to, hopefully, in a ten- or fifteen-minute conversation, connect the box of Venice Bakery pizza crust that was in their refrigerator to a real person. We wanted everyone who tried our pizza to say, "This is not just Venice Bakery. This comes from my *friend's* bakery. It's not just a name or company. These are real people that I can relate to, I can talk to, I can get emails from."

Trade shows helped us form and maintain that real connection with our customers: to get to know them, their spouses, how many kids they had, what stage in life their kids were in, whatever made them tick, whether it was football, basketball, aviation, whatever it was. We were interested.

I mean, I'd be at a damn roulette table with a customer who was doing $200,000 a week in sales with us until three in the morning, drinking Red Bull and having fun, and then still be at that tradeshow booth at 9:00 a.m. the next day. Going home after all of that, I was a mess, to be honest. But when you have the opportunity to be with such a valued customer, you take it. (One of those guys was from Nebraska. His name was John Steffens, and he and I are still good friends today even though I've been out of this business for seven years.)

I enjoyed those shows tremendously.

—Jimmy DeSisto

We did a minimum of three to four trade shows every year. There was a lot of taste-testing all day long...getting our food directly to the people who would then order it from their distributor was, again, a big key to our success. We had to get this product in the mouths of pizza lovers! A friend of mine explained it perfectly. He said, "No matter how good you are, if nobody knows about you, you will not be successful."

At first, not many people knew how good our pizza was, so we had to find a way to get it to the masses in a short period of time to stay ahead of the curve. There was one trade show that was our primary target, the International Pizza Expo held in March each year at the Las Vegas Convention Center. This is how we got our product into the number-one nationwide pizza chain, Domino's. All the biggest chains and retailers went to these shows with their buyers to source new products, better products, or trending products.

23

Sell More Crusts

At Venice Bakery in the mid-2010s, we didn't have any other products besides pizza crusts. We felt if we focused on the one thing we knew best, we would do well. We wanted to sell the absolute best product we could. Fortunately, the growth of our one product was robust because of market demand in this category and also because of the high quality we were offering.

As we became known as a high-quality, gluten-free co-packer, many companies approached us with all types of opportunities. Two companies approached us to consider producing products slightly outside of our domain: Girls Scouts of America to manufacture a gluten-free Girl Scout cookie and Olive Garden to manufacture gluten-free bread-sticks. Although we always hated to say no, we thought long and hard about these enormous opportunities and ultimately decided these two products were not in our wheelhouse and had to decline to be fair to both of those organizations. It was also the right thing to do so as not to take away from our focus on what we did best. We believed we could win by focusing on the one thing we specialized in perfecting: the best-tasting gluten-free pizza crust.

Udi's was owned by Smart Balance at the time (they ultimately changed their name to Boulder Brands), a big company out of Denver, Colorado, that offered a number of products in the marketplace. Helping realize that we were becoming a real player in this gluten-free pizza crust category was when we were approached by Udi's, which was then co-packing their line of gluten-free pizzas from a source other than us.

In 2012, while we were exhibiting at the National Restaurant Association Show in Chicago, *USA Today* published an article announcing that Domino's was now offering a gluten-free pizza option. That was the first national introduction to gluten-free pizza. This announcement was game-changing for us and the industry. Now that the country knew that the largest pizza chain in the world was carrying this trendy option, this category went mainstream. Word was quickly getting out to the industry that we were the manufacturers for them. Venice Bakery was instantly introduced to the world.

When Boulder Brands found this out, they sent their Smart Balance research team to find and meet with us. Since we were a white-label and private-label pizza manufacturing company, we weren't doing much advertising and marketing at that time, so we were not on everyone's radar and probably a bit difficult to locate in the small town of El Segundo. Remaining relatively out of sight was extremely beneficial for us up until that time, as it allowed us to quietly achieve our goals without outgrowing ourselves.

Two of their chief innovation officers, Peter Dray and David McCarthy, traveled to Venice, California, in an effort to find Venice Bakery. After a few days of research, they tracked us down in El Segundo. They called us and asked for a meeting with Jimmy and me. Obviously, we did not hesitate to set up one as quickly as possible. We were humbled to say the least.

They had their branded Udi's gluten-free pizza with them, so we did a side-by-side taste test. Although we were very confident in ourselves, it is always a bit nerve-wracking when you are doing a side-by-side comparison with someone who already believes in their own product. After the pizzas came out of the oven and we cut them up, we watched closely as they tasted both crusts alone, no toppings.

We saw them look at each other and say, "WOW!"

They were definitely impressed with our crusts.

Then, Peter turned to David and said, "Can you imagine if *this* pizza was in *our* box?"

Our gluten-free crust was clearly better than what they were offering. They wanted Venice to be a co-packer for Udi's fully topped gluten-free pizza. Even though we didn't have the capacity to put together a fully-topped pizza, we wanted to move forward. We saw this as a great opportunity—it was the first company with a known grocery store brand that showed interest in Venice for a co-packing opportunity. It was a big deal to us at the time.

Thus, we sought out a co-packer we could work with. KT's Kitchens was a prominent wheat-based topping facility located in Gardena, California. Many pizza manufacturers used KT's as a co-packer to top and box their pizza crusts; Venice Bakery and the DeSistos had in fact worked together in the past for several wheat-based projects and accounts. Once we secured the Udi's account in 2012, Jimmy and I met with Kathy Taggares, the owner of KT's Kitchens. Jimmy said, "Okay, here's the opportunity. Udi's loves our gluten-free crusts. Let's put together pricing for them for the full package."

After quite a bit of reluctance on her part, solely because she was not working with gluten-free products at the time and felt there would be too much cross-contamination, we let her know how we handled this concern by running gluten-free on certain days after sanitation days. Ultimately, we convinced Kathy to work with Udi's due to the potential of not only the gluten-free pizza market, but also more opportunities with their company. We worked out a plan in which we shipped the crusts to KT's, and they then spread the sauce, cheese, pepperoni, etc., and worked directly with Udi's from that point forward in the process.

Udi's was the first full pizza co-packing request, but definitely not the last. It got to the point where we had relationships like this with co-packers throughout the country. Another key topping facility we worked with was out of Nebraska: DI Manufacturing, run efficiently by John Steffens.

Udi's started out as a customer, and then not long after that—within a year—its parent company came back with the idea of acquiring us, which you'll read about shortly. While we weren't wrong to say yes to every opportunity early on, it was wise to start to focus our efforts as time passed. Our goal was simple: sell more crusts.

* * *

This basic understanding of what it took to be successful helped me with all of my businesses as I moved forward. I always applied the same formula to each of my subsequent ventures. Taking what I studied in school and then put into practice, I was able to transform that knowledge into action, which is where I saw real progress and success.

Having the ability to recognize one's talents and abilities is important when managing people. At Venice, we grew from approximately fifty employees to over 400 employees, and trying to keep everyone happy and help them grow professionally and individually was challenging, to say the least.

This was not always easy because we had such a family environment that the DeSistos had created. We knew we were responsible for our employees' families and took great pride in the positive environment we provided. For the most part, this was a mutually respectful relationship, which was a critical part of our success. Jimmy and I always said our company's organization chart pyramid was inverted—the employees represented the top, and Jimmy and I sat at the bottom. If our employees were unhappy, we had no idea if they were maintaining the quality of what was being made and packed. It was our job to empower the team.

This is a good point in the story to highlight the contributions of some of our stand-out employees. For example, our production manager, Martin Garcia, ran the plant for Jimmy (and for the family prior to Jimmy running the business). Martin was skilled at managing his people. He also had deep mechanical skills and the ability to solve production issues. If pizza wasn't coming out properly or there were problems in the production line, he had the innate ability to figure out why. Was the dough too wet? Was it the humidity in the proofer? Was the oven not set properly? He could tackle all those tasks because of his long-standing experience with production. As we continued to grow and took more of a science (as opposed to an art or instinct) approach with the gluten-free transition, there was a little bit of a learning curve, but he stayed committed.

We left Martin at the plant in El Segundo as we built out our new facility in Torrance, and he continued to run both wheat-based products and the little bit of gluten-free production we were doing in the original facility. He became educated and experienced with the gluten-free production techniques by trial and error. Needless to say, we trusted him to get things done.

Martin also had an assistant manager, Rojelio Pavon. Rojelio played an integral role as an assistant and was instrumental in our success. Rojelio also had a long-term relationship with the DeSistos and Venice Bakery.

As we continued to grow, our logistics and shipping department became an intricate part of the overall process. That department was run by Pedro Lozano. Our mechanical department consisted of Frank Aranda, the manager, and long-time employee Stan Bruner, who was with the family for years. Frank then brought on Kelly Komatsu. Kelly was an extremely knowledgeable mechanic and was able to add a major role in terms of leadership and education. Most of these employees are still there to this day. Clearly, we had built an entire infrastructure. They say that teamwork makes your dream work. Well, Jimmy and I had a great team.

* * *

The fast growth of Venice Bakery in the 2010s meant having to give up some responsibilities as we grew, especially at we were going. It was obvious that we needed to continue to scale through delegation. Prior to Venice, for instance, I always controlled staffing myself. The businesses I ran in Rhode Island were small enough that I could deal with any and all employee issues. Similarly, prior to 2010, Jimmy had handled all staffing and employee needs. As Venice started to grow, however, Jimmy and I knew this task was much more than we could handle alone. Thus, we hired a staffing agency to help handle all the human resources, staffing, and employee needs.

As an entrepreneur, you're used to making all the decisions and handling all facets of the business. Giving up control does not come easy. This is a common trait among successful entrepreneurs. However, giving up those controls actually benefited us. It allowed us to focus on what we did best: growing the business via sales and marketing.

24

A Real Player

Within a year of Venice working with KT's to supply pizza to Udi's, Peter and David came back and asked us out to dinner. The next day, we met in our offices, and they told us they wanted to make an offer to purchase Venice Bakery. This was the first offer that Jimmy and I received, and we were intrigued. They wanted to offer us $13 million in cash and stock. To both Jimmy and me, that was a lot of money. However, we needed to discuss the offer in depth. One of the main things we talked through was the uncertainty around the value of stock as part of the offer. Share prices can be so volatile that we weren't sure selling Venice for stock (even in part) would be the savvy move.

After much consideration, we respectfully declined. It was a tough decision, for sure, but we did not feel that it truly reflected our potential and long-term goals. The only way to make a good deal is if you are willing to say no and walk away. Which we were, and it was the right call. A quick bit of advice to any entrepreneur: don't get too excited about that first offer to buy your company. Let your initial emotions settle, and then look at the entirety of any offer calmly. Be sure you understand everything on the table, and do not underestimate the value of what you've built!

* * *

Jimmy and I were both in the business to grow it, yet we had no idea how *much* it was going to grow and how *fast* it was going to grow. As you've been reading, the gluten-free market took off like a rocket. And we were the gluten-free pizza guys. It wasn't until everybody else in the business saw how fast we were growing and how the demand was increasing that others started dipping their feet in too. Fortunately, we had such a giant head start by then that they had a long way to go.

You've got to have a great product, you've got to have the right people making the products, and then you've got to have excellent distribution. Relationship-building really mattered. When Jimmy went out to see Dot Foods in person, he noticed they had a staff of people sitting in cubicles fielding calls from all these different food service distributors, just taking orders. We knew that those people had to know who Venice Bakery was. We wanted them to know the products that we built and have the confidence to recommend us when that food service distributor called and said, "Hey, I need a gluten-free pizza crust."

We created a swag bag for them. In that bag were things you'd want to have at your desk—things like a picture frame for their favorite photo. Of course, that picture frame said Venice Bakery at the bottom. We created Venice Bakery water bottles, coffee cups, note pads, you name it. If you were sitting in a cubicle at Dot Foods, we wanted you to see the name Venice Bakery on everything. Also, when we had the chance to meet these people in person at trade shows, we had a pizza constantly coming out of the oven. So when the Dot people came and sat with us, Jimmy started to form that bond and made sure they had a chance to try the product and get to know us personally, as real people. That human connection and those real relationships are everything.

Once we were well-established with Dot, it made it so much easier for us at trade shows. There was no place we couldn't ship to now, and if the end-user did not meet our minimum order to come directly to us, they could simply order with their distributor, who would then order from Dot. While it may sound like we were putting all our eggs in one basket, that wasn't the case. Even after we started working with Dot, companies could still order directly with us, as long as they met our minimum orders of half a truckload or more. Dot gave us the ability to scale faster with their model to service all the independent foodservice distributors. Since end users did not have any minimum orders to meet, Dot helped us in streamlining production runs and keeping costs down. Working with them contributed to a win-win situation for all.

* * *

To most entrepreneurs, setting up a pizza crust manufacturing line or signing with another product distributor like Dot is not relevant to your concerns. I get it. However, understanding that we needed to increase capacity because of the growing demand is the key takeaway here. The law of supply and demand is a factor in every business.

Evaluating whether the decisions we made and the risks we took were worth the reward was very challenging. How do you assess risk? You do it by gathering as much information as you can; you do it by identifying the obstacles; you do it by evaluating the likelihood of a reward; you do it by assessing the potential impact; and then you take action.

Guinness World Record

Prior to phasing out the wheat-based side of our business, there was one more challenge that we had to undertake. It all began when the director of Pizzaovens.com, Fash Asvadi, reached out with a crazy idea: to create the longest pizza ever made and secure a place in the Guinness World Records. It was a challenge we could not pass up! After gathering a team of industry professionals, Jimmy went to work. What followed were months of detailed planning and intense coordination.

The team faced a host of logistical challenges: how to design a conveyor belt large enough to handle such a massive pizza, whether to lay it out in a straight line or an oval shape, and how to ensure the oven could cook the pizza evenly. The scale of the operation also meant calculating vast quantities of ingredients—dough, sauce, cheese, and more—while timing every stage to perfection.

To break the world record held by Italy of 1.15 miles, the team set a new target: a pizza measuring 1.3 miles. With the right team in place, an incredible oven custom-built for the task, and meticulous planning, we were ready to make history. The oven itself, built on wheels, was designed to move outside the conveyor belt. It literally picked up the pizza on the belt as it cooked. The event took place in June 2017 at the Fontana Raceway in California.

Teams from Pizzaovens.com, Venice Bakery, Orlando Foods, and pizzaiolos Tony Gemignani, Giulio Adriani, and John Arena, among other partners, worked tirelessly to bring the vision to life. Over the course of fifty-four hours, and using approximately 17,700 pounds of dough supplied by Venice Bakery, 5,000 pounds of tomato sauce, and 3,900 pounds of mozzarella cheese, the record-breaking pizza measuring 6,333 feet, 3.6 inches was assembled and cooked. Afterwards, sections of it were sent out to local churches, shelters, and food banks within a twenty-mile radius, ensuring that the record-breaking pizza was shared with those in need.

Though the task seemed impossible at times, the team never gave up, and the world record was successfully achieved. To this day, the team's creation holds the Guinness World Record for the longest pizza ever made. The challenge was a monumental feat, and the effort remains a proud achievement for all involved.

25

Big Offers, Big Growth

A year after we were approached by the Boulder Brands group, a meat-processing company out of Chicago called Fontanini Meats came into the picture. A wholesale meat supplier, they were a dominant player in food service as both a manufacturer and distributor. We had a good relationship with the owner, Gene Fontanini. At the time, they didn't sell pizza, but they wanted to provide their clients with more products. In June of 2014, they requested to schedule a meeting at our offices in El Segundo.

Gene and his wife visited us that summer and we all went to lunch locally. Afterward, we went back to our offices and started to discuss their interest in acquiring Venice Bakery. They already knew our product well, so they were fully prepared to present an offer.

They made us an all-cash offer of $23 million.

Gene had already met with his bankers, so he knew the maximum number he could offer. We knew there was no negotiating or counteroffer that he would accept. Like the Boulder Brands offer, this was a lot of money to Jimmy and me, and we were very appreciative. Yet, we didn't see a lot of synergy between a meat supplier and a gluten-free pizza crust manufacturer.

After a lot of consideration, Jimmy and I decided that, in the best interest of both parties, this was not an offer we could accept. Similarly to the Boulder Brands offer, we weren't convinced that this deal would have aligned with our long-term goals of continuing to expand the company and keep control while doing so.

* * *

Getting offers to buy the business had started a year earlier and was both exciting and all-consuming. So all-consuming, in fact, that I had taken conference calls the morning after my wedding because we were being presented with potential buyers who were throwing out big numbers at us. We had all our friends and family from Rhode Island waiting for me to come down from the hotel room to have breakfast together, and I was on the phone.

Everybody we knew was there in the lobby of the Ritz-Carlton, and I was excusing myself repeatedly. I didn't know the right thing to do. It was overwhelming. Should I pay attention to the attorneys who were calling? If I didn't, would we lose the deal? Was I being rude to my family and friends who had trekked 3,000 miles to celebrate one of the best days of my life with us? It was a very bittersweet moment.

Those calls did not lead to a sale right then. But the way I handled them reflected my loyalty, my dedication to Jimmy. My role at Venice was execution—not just in production and manufacturing, but in all facets of the business. I felt an obligation to execute in all areas, and that included an acquisition. So, when these offers came in, Jimmy relied on me to deal with them. Sure, he could have dealt with any and all issues, but for me, there was a sense of responsibility to some degree. I'm not so sure it was fair to Carla or everybody else that weekend, but I think they understood. They may not even remember it, but I do.

* * *

In 2016, one of the largest private-label, family-owned food manufacturers in the U.S., Rich Products, headquartered in Buffalo, New York, contacted us inquiring about the possibility of an acquisition.

Kevin Malchoff, a board member who was in charge of Global Development, came out to see us and toured the El Segundo facility. He was extremely impressed with the operation and how we were able to maximize every square inch of the floor. As a result, Kevin reported his positive impressions to his team in Buffalo. The company then came back out to visit us with five senior executives, important decision-makers. One of them was a new division leader named Donna Reeves. She was an accomplished category leader in other industries and a valuable addition to their company. Donna walked the floor, clearly thinking through how our operation could be optimized using their resources.

This is when things started to get a little serious. We all went to dinner locally here in Manhattan Beach. It was a very productive and entertaining evening. The next day, we all met at our offices to discuss business and their interest in Venice. Their team presented us with the largest offer at that time, an astonishing $35 million, and it was all cash. This was larger than the expected offer. We were blown away, to say the least.

Jimmy and I sat in the office discussing this in-depth, talking about the pros and cons. I remember Carla coming into the office at that time. We told her what Rich's had just presented us with, and her foresightful response was, "I don't think you guys should sell. My gut tells me you will have a $100 million company if you keep working hard."

I don't know what kind of crystal ball she had, but I believed her.

Jimmy and I were incredibly surprised and deeply thankful for the generous offer, realizing how it could have changed our lives. After several days of thinking about this, we recognized the potential impact on our lives and our families. At the same time, we believed we still had room to grow. And grow big. We had recently purchased the Torrance building and were in the process of installing our new lines. We realized the potential of that building and were still eager to expand the business as much as possible on our own. So, without further consideration, Jimmy and I made the very difficult decision to respectfully decline.

* * *

From 2010 to 2013, our work focused on bringing awareness to, and growing, the gluten-free category. From 2013 on, it was about meeting demand—doing more of what we were already doing well. When it came time to build out our fourth production line, we had reached maximum capacity with our first two lines in Torrance and our capacity in El Segundo, yet the demand was still there, and our building in Torrance had room for one last line. We knew we couldn't use VTech for a new oven, of course. (Lesson learned the hard way.)

We wanted a design and engineering firm to work with all of the equipment pieces and put them together even more efficiently than we had done in-house with our third line. So, we hired another company to design the line layout and source the manufacturers for each production line piece. However, once again, we hit a roadblock: this line was not working well once it was up and running. We could not get the oven temperature to the specs we needed. We had several consultants in to help us diagnose the problem, and they found the oven needed a lot of work. At that point, we had to almost remanufacture the oven while it was on the floor in line.

Months and thousands of working hours later, we were able to get the oven to a working condition, but there were still issues with that line. As efficient as we expected it to be compared to the previous lines, we weren't seeing any greater output. There should have been a noticeable product volume increase.

Rich Products, our ultimate buyer, had a full engineering team as well as deep relationships with equipment manufacturers, so they knew they could address any and all problems. What they really needed from us was our recipe, our proprietary step-by-step production process, our customers, and the expertise of Venice's leadership (Jimmy and myself).

26

Rich Products

In the end, all business operations can be
reduced to three words: people, product, and
profits. People come first.
—Lee Iacocca

Though we'd entertained and respectfully declined three
different offers to buy the company, Jimmy and I were not
averse to the idea that selling Venice Bakery might be the
right move. By 2016, we saw growth potential as a reason to
sell, meaning we thought the business could grow stronger
and faster with a buyer's resources and scale, as long as there

was clear synergy. When we met with potential buyers, we weighed the pros and cons of each one.

Things shifted quite a bit in 2016. That year, we were getting solicited by bankers who specialized in mergers and acquisitions and wanted to take us to the next level in terms of the purchase price and overall terms. There must have been some chatter out in the industry that we were not aware of. Once we heard that we had several interested parties who wanted to talk to us about a sale, we needed to learn more about the process. I contacted our CPAs, Jeff Richardson and Christian Emerson, from the firm Richardson, Kontogouris, and Emerson (a.k.a. RKE). Jeff and Christian then referred us to a law firm, Buchalter Nemer. We worked with partners Tanya Viner and Jeremy Weitz. After discussing it further, we knew we needed to find the right investment bankers to represent us as well.

We met with Spartan Group, based in Los Angeles, and Houlihan Lokey, a publicly traded company in Chicago. After a careful vetting process, we ultimately signed with Houlihan. Not only did we mesh well with their style, but we also felt that as a publicly traded company, they could attract a high-caliber buyer.

Jimmy and I, along with our controller Brian Khoddam, put together a pitch deck. Throughout the process, which took months, we came up with an exciting and intriguing deck. Houlihan then took it to several interested parties. They set up meetings with three private equity groups and two strategic buyers. One of them, which they had worked with in the past, was Rich Products. Funny how things come full circle.

This process of meeting with potential buyers lasted for months. It was a lengthy and delicate process requiring patience and good negotiating skills. Houlihan guided us the whole way. We were promoting the company's core principles and long-term goals in order to determine which buyer had the same long-term vision and the best interest of the company and our employees. Taking care of our employees—our extended family—was an important factor in our decision. The buyers were also doing their due diligence, assessing our entire business, including our customer base, our operations, and our financials, and aligning their strategic interests. I must say, there were times the sale seemed near, yet either stalled or fell through.

Though we'd turned down the earlier $35-million offer from Rich Products, they emerged as the best strategic fit for us by far. They operated worldwide, they had their own distribution and logistics arms, and they encompassed a global sales team. We were still considered a small company based on the traditional definition of "small" as it is measured by sales, yet we had the largest share of the overall gluten-free pizza category in the marketplace.

Rich Products made us the most substantial offer, but we didn't choose them simply because their offer was the biggest. We chose Rich Products because they were the best strategic partner. We knew if anybody was going to take this company to another level *and* respect our staff, our team, and the family environment we were building, it would be them. During this time, they really wooed us with their hospitality. Jimmy and I flew to their headquarters in Buffalo on a private jet and saw our names on the sign welcoming us to their family. In conversation, it was obvious they wanted to learn and understand who we were as individuals. They asked questions like, "Where are you from? "What do you like to do personally? Do you have hobbies? What got you into this business?" They cared.

* * *

One of the reasons Rich Products was aggressive in pursuing us even after our initial "no" was because of the cuttings that we kept winning ("cuttings" are defined as taste tests). Competitors kept losing to this little company called Venice Bakery. The whole time we thought we were chasing this behemoth worldwide company making gluten-free pizza at scale, it turned out they were chasing *us*.

Rich Products had done their research to find out who we were, what we were doing, and who our customers were, yet they could not figure out how we were making such a premium product. We didn't know all of our competition; we just knew it was extremely limited.

Our competitors were chasing us in this category simply because gluten-free pizza was the core of our business, and as a result, we had mastered our domain. As I wrote in the introduction, people at trade shows jokingly nicknamed us the "Google boys of gluten-free pizza" because we were dominant players and growing so quickly. Our market share was increasing year over year at a noticeable rate. The bankers negotiated our purchase price to a number that was eye-opening for us. It was based on documented success (historical earnings), run rate (estimated earnings), and a value placed on these metrics. This value is determined by multiplying a certain number (called a multiple that is negotiated by both parties) times our EBITDA (Earnings Before Interest, Taxes, Depreciation, and Amortization).

We went out to the Rich's headquarters in Buffalo, New York, for the last time and sat down with about twenty people, including managers, supervisors, and the whole pizza leadership team, which included Bill Gisel, Executive Vice Chairman; Richard Ferrari, CEO; Donna Reeves, who ran the pizza category by then; and David Faturos, Chief Financial Officer. At one point, they pulled Jimmy aside to be sure everyone's intentions were aligned on both sides. Obviously they were, so the deal moved forward. Their internal and external legal team worked with Tanya and Jeremy of Buchalter Nemer to finalize the details of the deal, which was signed on Thursday, November 30, 2017.

* * *

Exiting the business came at us fast. It was an emotional consideration as well as a financial consideration. Jimmy had two boys he initially thought would take over the business; however, after thinking about the pros and cons of siblings working together, and reflecting on the experiences we'd both had with our own brothers, he felt that selling Venice Bakery was the best decision for all in the long run. We would both be in a position to take care of our families and spend more time with them. Time is something money can't buy.

To others in our shoes, I'd say it is important to think through all considerations when an exit opportunity is presented: Is it the right time? Research market conditions and review growth opportunities within the company. Check your growth against the competition, and be sure you understand the mergers and acquisitions market in terms of interest rate impact. Then, pursue all options. If an exit strategy is what you choose, interview bankers, legal representation, and financial representation. Lastly, prepare for life after the sale. Have a plan both personally and professionally.

When I came into the business in 1994, there were people at Venice Bakery who had already been working for maybe fifteen or sixteen years in the business who knew my grandfather. They were all from Mexico and Central America. I knew when I got into the business that I better learn how to speak Spanish, so I forced myself to listen to cassette tapes in my car. Driving from El Segundo to Costa Mesa where I lived, all I did was listen to those tapes. My Spanish got pretty good.

As time went on, some Venice Bakery employees exited because of the growth, but most of them stayed. The deal with Rich Products almost blew up pertaining to employees, actually. In the ninth inning of our deal, another bakery business was raided in Chicago by immigration services, and all the employees ran. It shut that bakery down, and it made Rich look at us under a microscope, checking on the status of all of our employees.

We had done what we were required to do according to California employment law. As we grew, the HR aspects of the business became a real headache. Joe and I made the decision to outsource all the employees to a third-party agency.

We had to let all the people know, "Yes, you are still part of this Venice Bakery family. However, your paycheck is now going to be coming from this particular third-party entity."

When Rich Products came to us after the raid at the Chicago bakery, they said, "We're not sure we can go through with this deal because of the way you guys have hired your employees." We made it perfectly clear that they weren't just buying this company; they had to take care of everyone who worked for us as well. Because no matter how big a deal is, if you can't turn your back on it and walk away and let other people know you're going to walk away, you have no power. You might as well let them run the whole show.

We let them know, "We're good either way. We'll continue to do what we're doing; we will continue to compete with you in this world of gluten-free. But if you want to buy us, we need to have peace of mind that our people are going to be protected."

At the end of the day, they decided to proceed with the deal, but they asked for a million dollars to be held back for one year just in case a situation arose with employee status. Joe and I were confident that we had followed all rules and regulations, so we agreed. Fortunately, nothing negative happened to anyone.

The message during the buyout period to all the employees was this: You're working under this umbrella of Venice Bakery, and we want to move you all under the umbrella of Rich Products that looks much bigger—and involves the resources and benefits that are going to come with that bigger umbrella. As a result of this shift, if we need to hire attorneys, that's just fine. We are in for whatever we need to do to help you get your status to be able to remain under this big umbrella.

Many legacy employees are still there today, working under Rich's umbrella. For the most part, our people were happy. That's stepping up the ladder of life...not stepping on people to get there, but carrying people with you.

—Jimmy DeSisto

27

"Is This For Real?"

During the summer of 2017, the negotiation processes to sell Venice Bakery had started in earnest. It started a very stressful few months. Once back home from our summer vacation, I started to feel ill and wasn't sure what it was. It turned out I had shingles in my throat! That's a very uncommon place to get shingles. Needless to say, it was difficult to eat, speak, or swallow. As a result, I was forced to miss some of the initial meetings with bankers and the potential buyers because all I could do was rest. Jimmy attended the meetings with our controller, Brian, who did a good job of sharing the documents and discussing financials, while Jimmy did a great job addressing the history and the ambitions of the company, as well as all other sales-related questions anyone had.

When it came to other related parts of the business, the buyers had lots of questions for me as they related to operations, infrastructure, and growth plans. Since these folks were flying in from all over the country expecting answers to their questions there and then, I feel that some of them were less tolerant of my absence than others. I do know it had an impact on some of the folks at Rich's, as they let me know later on. Some of their folks were concerned with my health and my ability to sustain my role in the long term. Others in their organization expressed their sympathy since they themselves had experienced this condition in the past.

* * *

It was overwhelming not knowing what to expect during this time of transition and change. The unknown was the big thing causing us stress. We were going into these meetings with the bankers while the interested parties had a whole team, sometimes up to seven people on their other side of the table who had been through these processes before. We had never done anything like it, so we were taking advice and listening to our bankers who, fortunately, were seasoned veterans.

We knew at the end of the day, you've got to trust your gut. This has held true for my whole career, and Jimmy was extremely intuitive as well. After meeting with all these groups, Jimmy and I went back to our homebase in Torrance to discuss who we felt would be the best buyer. All of our professional teams were able to shed light on the process and express their feelings, but the ultimate decision was up to Jimmy and me. Our gut led us to make the decision to move forward with Rich Products.

It was important to us that our buyer would maintain the business so all the people we had employed would keep their jobs. Likewise, the Rich folks were adamant about keeping Jimmy and me in the business after the sale. The contingency was that we both stayed on for three years to help with the transition. They ended up coming back to us and asked us to remain in our roles for five years. In return, they offered us a worthwhile bonus for those additional two years.

Before agreeing, we talked it out, and I remember saying to Jimmy, "You know, why not? If they're going to make it worthwhile for us to do this for two more years, let's do it. We're never going to make that amount of money at this stage in our life somewhere else in such a short period of time."

Those last two years were tied to earnings, while the first three were put in place just to help the business transition to being part of a larger ecosystem. We were extremely confident we could get the earnings up to target within that period. We were betting on ourselves. After three years, we got there! Rich had set up the entire business the way they wanted it. They incorporated corporate controls so their main office was able to look at remote production and all financials. (They implemented manufacturing software back in their main office in Buffalo as well as at the operation in Torrance that made this possible.)

After three years, they came to us in December of 2020 and said, "Listen, we will pay you your total earnout including salary for the next two years, health benefits for the next two years, and continue to contribute to the 401k, but in exchange, we would like control now."

Originally, we had been able to negotiate in our employment contracts that anything that had to do with gluten-free pizza had to pass through us first—if we were responsible for that category, and our bonus was tied to performance, we needed to have the final say.

During that year-end call in December 2020, I thought, *Is this for real? Are they really going to pay us our bonus and not require us to work for the remaining two years?*

I immediately called our attorney Tanya, and we redrafted the employment agreement to make sure what they were requesting and offering was very clear on both sides.

I had reached my goal of retiring at fifty-five.

* * *

When it was all said and done, when it was actually time to walk away from the business, it was surreal. However, because we maintained ownership of all our real estate, we were always in touch with the team at Rich Products, even after all of our obligations to them were fulfilled. They were great buyers in every way…a great company full of terrific people. They kept all our employees in place as they had promised, which was extremely important to us. We felt we were responsible for feeding so many families; the last thing we wanted to do was take food off their plates. The folks at Rich had no intention of disrupting those relationships. In fact, they welcomed that continuity, and were true to their word that it would be maintained. Yes, they streamlined some things and some people did leave. But it was not an overhaul of the Venice Bakery company in any way.

Our success was achieved by working hard and working smart. Taking risks and never looking back, only forward. We didn't care what anyone else was doing in the world of pizza. We were the leaders, the most innovative pizza company on the planet, taking our slice of a forty-five-billion-dollar market.

The only way you learn what it takes is by doing it… by having the opportunity to start a business, grow a business, and sell a business. Most people will never know. The goal in life is to one day have your money work for you. Not you working for your money.

Nothing comes easy in this game. There are going to be trials and tribulations and tough times; blood, sweat, and tears in anything you do to be successful. Build good relationships around you. You'll need them to be able to build a company in any type of structure, whether it's selling a widget or selling a service.

You have to be different, create something that's unique, and work really, really hard. Most people just want to have that paycheck to be able to survive. Most people choose the safe route. A lot of people are just looking to be comfortable, and that paycheck at the end of the week makes them comfortable.

Finally, you can't micromanage, and you cannot be greedy. Don't ever make a product based on money; make a product based on it being the greatest product out there. The food distributors, who would get upset with us because we wouldn't participate in their marketing programs, would say, "Hey, if you're not going to participate in this marketing program, we're not going to be able to sell your product anymore."

And we'd respond, "We get it. We understand that. But your competitor is selling our product. And if you don't bring it to the end user, they will."

Having the greatest product in the marketplace was powerful for us. But we didn't exude that power in a way that was disrespectful. It was simply known.

Now that we've sold the business, I wouldn't say we're retired now. It was time to sell, and the opportunity that presented itself was right. There's one thing money can't buy, and that's time. Selling the business gave us the time to watch our children grow, and there's no greater gift.

—Jimmy DeSisto

Reflection

As a young kid from the biggest little state in the Union, I never thought I could help run a business worth hundreds of millions of dollars. Yet once we got to those roundtables, sitting across from these large private equity groups and other companies that were saying, "We want you because you've done a good job," I started to reflect on the history of getting to that point. My doubts and insecurities started to fade because I had learned that even when you feel scared or have doubts, it helps to take action. Stay in the game, do things, and face those fears. It *is* scary. It's very scary at times. But that's extremely normal.

Even if you fail, it is okay if you try to learn from it. The drive that you have inside will force you to get up and do something in a different way. As you move forward, let others enhance your own skills and abilities. For example, in the eighties when I sold my lemonade business after college and moved back to Rhode Island, I started a sponsored softball team. I called up my friends, including Eddie Mulvey, probably one of the best natural athletes I have ever played with. He was the type of kid where if the bases were loaded, you would walk him because you feared what he could do. He made everybody around him better. I was a good athlete, but compared to him, I was not even in the same league. The point is, when you surround yourself with people like that, you naturally become better yourself. Eddie did that to people. Cherish the Eddies you meet; they're something special, and they'll make you better.

When you're younger and seizing an opportunity, you also have to believe in *yourself*, even if you have some small lingering doubts or insecurities. If you don't believe in yourself, no one else is going to believe in you. As long as you have integrity and are passionate about what you want to do, find a way to do that better than everyone else. Money will always follow. I came out to California on a handshake with Jimmy, truly not making a lot of money my first year. He knew that my execution was unstoppable, and I was all in; I did not have a backup plan. The rewards came as a result of hard work, passion, and dedication.

* * *

After the sale, the Rich Products people then told me they had been concerned with my illness to the point where they almost pulled out of the deal. However, I had no idea during the meetings with them at the time.

I learned this concern was significant because after the sale, two executives personally called me to tell me the acquisition was a package deal; if I wasn't going to stay on to help with the transition, they were out. They were not going to buy the business. They said that they were impressed with my contribution to the growth of the company and clearly recognized and valued my role. This truly validated what I brought to the table. This was the moment I realized my true worth to the company: the value of my contribution and years of hard work and dedication.

If I had never had shingles, I never would have gotten the insight and validation from the folks at Rich about how valuable I truly was to the business. How much my work mattered. Now, I carry that with me, and I'm grateful. As terrible as it was to go through that obstacle at such a crucial time in the business, it did give me that gift. Recognizing the fact that others who did not know me put so much value on my work and accomplishments was reassuring.

I came out here to California to work hard and seize an opportunity given to me. And fortuitously for us, the gluten-free market took off bigger than any of our expectations. Then the cauliflower product that followed—the second generation of gluten-free pizza crust—absolutely smashed it. It was a home run straight over the centerfield wall. When the sale finally went through, we knew what had happened was life-changing.

28

Fatherhood

Carla and I knew we wanted to have children. However, we were not sure when the right time would be. We were both getting older, enjoying life, and traveling quite a bit. Ultimately, we asked ourselves, *How do we enhance our life together even further?* When we were going through the sale of the business, that's when we made the decision.

I looked at Carla and said, "If we're going to have a child, I think this is the time. I want to have the energy to spend with him or her and give them the best childhood that we possibly can."

Fortunately, the gods were with us, and we were blessed with a quick pregnancy. We were both convinced it was a boy. After coming home from a meeting in Detroit with the Domino's folks, Carla and her Mom sat me down. She put a cupcake in front of me with pink and blue balloons tied to the chair. She had been to the doctor that day and found out the gender of the baby. When I cut through the cupcake, it was pink! I could not believe it! I remember getting chills and this sense of happiness I had never felt before. "We're having a girl!" I said in amazement.

Luckily, the pregnancy and birth went smoothly…no health issues at all. Carla delivered our daughter Audrey Rose on May 10 of 2018, which was a remarkable coincidence because the only license plate my father ever had included the number 510. My dad passed away six weeks later…I still get choked up when I think about the fact that he never got a chance to meet her. Today in memory of him, I still have the only license plate he ever had, which reflects the date of Audrey's birth, 510.

Dad, I know you will never get the chance to read this, but I want to tell you how thankful I am for all you've done for me. You were more than a dad to me for my entire life. You guided me, taught me, and inspired me like no one else could. Your wisdom, your patience, and your strength were always there helping me become who I am today.

I aim to follow your example and become that type of dad to Audrey.

* * *

We went home from the hospital two days later, ironically on Mother's Day. Even though I wasn't sure I could change diapers, I did. I was hands-on from the beginning.

Carla was, as all moms are, the strong one…the one that played a bigger role as I was still working as part of the sale agreement.

More recently, it's been amazing to bring our daughter to school, to pick her up and to go to all of her activities, to play with her, even when she wants to play with dolls and princesses…it's all great to me. We are truly present in everything she does and dedicated to raising a polite, respectful, and well-mannered young lady.

Audrey has always been in tune with everything going on around her. I remember when she was six months old and doing her first Mommy and Me swim class, there was another woman watching on the side of the pool with me and asked, "Is that your daughter?" I replied, "Yeah," and she said, "I work with a lot of kids. Your child knows her surroundings already. She just knows where everybody is. She is going to be a very intelligent young girl."

* * *

When we decided to have our first child, I said at the time, "If we're going to have one, we're having two." I grew up in a big family. I didn't realize it doesn't always happen like it did with Audrey. It can be pretty difficult.

The second time we tried to conceive, we went through quite a bit of work. It took us two or three years to exhaust all our options until it was determined that this was not going to be possible.

Carla and I took this as a sign that we were going to be happy with the one child we have and it was meant to be.

My dearest Audrey Rose,

I met your dad at the age of eighteen. I sit and write this note to you at fifty-eight. Wow, forty years later in what seems to be a blink of an eye. By the time you read this book, you will have already realized you hit the Daddy Lottery. We don't have the same bloodlines, but I feel blessed to have been adopted into your family, and for you to call me Uncle Jimmy. There's no doubt God brought your dad and me together as we needed each other in this game of life.

You're blessed to have role-model parents and be raised in a home where Mom and Dad love each other. And guess what? Your Uncle Jimmy loves you more than you could ever imagine. I love you and love watching you grow.

—Jimmy DeSisto

29

The Netflix Show

I find myself going back to everything I've experienced personally and professionally as I discuss my career, my life, and even this book with friends. What stands out to most people is how many businesses I've started or ran in my lifetime, considering my highs and lows— and how unusual that is for a small-town boy from a middle-class family. (Not to mention how noteworthy it is for someone who survived an FBI raid and life-threatening medical setbacks, including a brain tumor, to bounce back and succeed.) Something I hear fairly often is, "My gosh, this should be a Netflix show!"

After my young lemonade start-up, I ventured into a bureaucratic world with GMAC. Then, I was in the restaurant business with my dad. Next came the mortgage business, the home improvement business, and the software/casino business with my brother. There was also the salon and spa and the loan modification business. Ultimately, I went to Venice Bakery, and today I'm involved in various projects as a consultant and real estate owner/investor.

When I set out to write this book, I planned to mainly cover the seven years we grew the new gluten-free category. I wanted to build a bridge for my daughter, to show where I'd come from and how we got to where we are today. But as I wrote, these pages accumulated over time to tell the full story of what came before those seven years. I discovered that my earlier life experiences had provided a valuable foundation for what we accomplished at Venice Bakery. The speed with which we grew that business was based on the fact that both Jimmy and I had learned a few things ahead of time—things that could've *only* been absorbed through experiences, both good and bad, via triumph and failure, and by trial and error.

People ask me, "How did you figure out all of these different things?"

Opportunities will come for all of us throughout life. Are you ready to take advantage of these opportunities? This preparation comes from your own resilience. There will be many things that come up that we can not control. But how do you bounce back and handle these things? This is the difference. The people that succeed are the ones that have the grit and resilience inside of them and are ready to take advantage of the opportunities when they come our way.

Hone in on your ability to put all the pieces together. No, it's not easy. I was driving the truck, setting up the hotdog cart, and figuring out marketing, for example. As any business grows, predict what is needed to get to the next step. Sometimes your predictions are correct, and sometimes, they're not. But the biggest decision successful people make is to try or not.

You cannot succeed if you do not try.

If you feel called to start a business, begin with the fundamentals. Start with a business plan. Show how you think this idea is different from what else is out there. What are you planning on doing to make this better so it is successful? Be consistent. Some of the biggest and best businesses were started with little to no money, so that's not the main factor. Instead, any business requires research, discipline, and execution. You may fail, which is okay. You learn more from failure than you do from success. Do it young. You will have more time to make it up later.

People fail to take action because they fear the unknown, but it's possible to stack the odds in your favor. There is a difference between risks and calculated risks. Do the work; do the math, and then take action. Successful entrepreneurs understand that risk is unavoidable. So take the time to understand it, prepare for it, and adjust as needed. I have a friend I've known for probably thirty years. And for thirty years, he has said, "I want to buy a home in Florida. I can't stand these East Coast winters."

Now, after finally buying that property in Florida, he realizes it is the happiest thing he has ever done. He's fifty years old, and he is now saying, "Oh, I should've done this earlier." If you continue to wait until you are ready, you will be waiting for the rest of your life.

My goal of retiring at fifty-five? I didn't know that was going to happen, but I had to have a set goal because it made me work hard. It pushed me hard to get there. I feel blessed and thankful as a result. Now I don't feel guilty traveling when I want to travel, taking time off when I want to take time off, and spending as much time as I can with my daughter, all what I worked so hard to do.

* * *

Before the business was sold, Joe had a vision of helping his family pay off mortgages and college expenses.

I'll be honest, I talked to him about it because I wanted to be sure he wanted to do this. It was an extremely generous offer. When this all happened and the business sold, one of our bankers turned to us and said, "I've been doing this for almost twenty years, and I've never seen such unselfishness and generosity to that many people."

Joe goes above and beyond when it comes to taking care of everyone around him. In addition to all those tuition fees, he also paid off his younger sister's mortgage. She had a stroke in her early twenties, so she's not able to work and lives a difficult life. When the banker asked why Joe chose to do this, he got teary; he couldn't even speak about it. That's the kind of heart this man has.

I asked his sister to write a letter to Audrey to explain the kind of man that her dad is. Because when he sold the company, he wasn't thinking about just himself. I was! I was thinking about our little family. But he was thinking beyond that.

—Carla Tedeschi

The ups and downs throughout my life were wild, so it was never my intention while writing this book to list out my successes or accomplishments. The story was much more balanced than that.

When I was intimidated by playing sports with older, bigger kids, Dad would reassure me. *You might be smaller. You might be shorter. You might not be as big as others. But that doesn't mean you're not as good as they are.*

You can take risks in your life. How do you identify the risks worth taking? There is no secret formula. You just have to try. No one's going to do it for you, so when something inside of you is saying "yes," then do it.

Were we lucky to capitalize on the gluten-free demand? Some could say that, but we also took the risk to be ready for it *before* that trend matured. We took the risk of going all in at that moment, pursuing what we believed would be a forever-lasting trend: the gluten-free world. Nobody else wanted to do it, yet everybody else *could* have tried. For us, it was a matter of believing in the value of offering a delicious gluten-free food product, knowing that we could have failed. We happened to get lucky *after* we made the decision to take the risk, which put us in a position to capitalize on that well-timed decision. And it wasn't all about being lucky. The rest of the puzzle was completed thanks to hard work and the commitment we made to see it through.

I see too many people get complacent, and I understand it because I can get complacent too. It's easy for me to say, I can't do this, I can't do that. But I get strong mentally and do those things for my future with intent and motivation for the long term. I firmly believe that if you want something and try hard enough, you will get it. There are so many success stories like mine. Did everybody go through a brain tumor? No, but everybody has their own ups and downs.

When I was eighteen years old, I didn't know I'd be successful. But I did know that I would try, and try hard.

* * *

Creating this path in life alone can be difficult, but the journey will make you stronger. In every part of my life, I've had to carve out roads that were not easy. Lying in bed with my head wrapped from the brain surgery was hard, but it definitely made me stronger. The goal to attend USC on my own? Tough, tough, tough. When I jumped on that plane to California as an eighteen-year-old kid, I did not know anybody. I had no idea how to even find my seat! But taking that risk paid off, and it made me stronger.

Coming back to Connecticut for a semester was also a hard choice. That path was difficult, but I knew the decision to go back to USC would make my life better in the long term. Returning to California in 2010 to help Jimmy? There was no definitive end, no guarantee. But that choice, that road, is what made me braver. Given all of this, my message to my daughter is very important: *It's not going to be easy.* A lot of these choices are going to be hard. But they'll make you courageous. And never forget that I will support you till the end.

Hard Work Meets Good Luck

Understand the value of hard work. I was in the office at 6 a.m. every weekday and left at 6 p.m....good twelve-hour days, plus a lot of Saturdays. This doesn't count the endless hours thinking about the business, which is typical for a successful entrepreneur. Some people might say, "You guys were lucky. You were in the right space at the right time."

To that I would reply, sure, there's always an element of luck. But the more interesting question is, "How can we put ourselves in a position to capitalize on those situations that come our way?"

I've found a lot of common elements in my successful peers and associates, such as having a good, manageable routine. You need to be disciplined; have a schedule. Get up before your competitors, plan your day, and exercise. Start your consistent routine. If you want to stay ahead of everybody, you need to be in the thick of things, working hard. Keep a clear head so you can make intelligent decisions.

As I noted earlier in the book, when I was trying out for the scout team at USC, I would go out to the beach every night and run because what I had going for me was speed… my single advantage in terms of getting looked at. The only way I could lean into that advantage was to practice continuously, routinely. That mindset—that commitment—carried through in everything I've done.

Sadly, many young adults today rely on others to do things for them. No one will come and save you; your life is 100% your responsibility. Opportunities don't always fall in your lap. You have to seek them out and work to capitalize on them. The best things in life don't come easy. Not only do you have to be passionate about whatever it is you choose to pursue, but you also have to find something in life that you want to be better at than everyone else—be consistent, be determined, and work as hard as you can. I can't stress those things enough.

30

Acceptance

Of course there is no formula for success
except, perhaps, an unconditional
acceptance of life and what it brings.
—Arthur Rubenstein

This bears repeating one more time: my father always made me feel that it was okay to make mistakes. He was always there to love me. This helped me not to be afraid of taking risks because I knew I could always go home or always call home and still be loved. This is what I want to pass along to my daughter.

While growing up, I heard many people preach that the key to surviving each day was positivity. As I got older, I learned that the key was more about acceptance. Some days will be bad. Some days will be good. Everything is not always going to be perfect; however, accepting the good and the bad is the important thing to surviving. Once you do, you can deal with what life throws at you. Remember that strong times don't last, but strong people do. My joke about this is to ask people if they can tell I only have half my organs: No appendix, no gallbladder, only one eye, and half a brain! (Ha.)

Work towards enjoying each day. Work towards doing what you love to do in life. Don't chase money. As long as you are doing what you love to do, money will follow. If you end up working for money, you will not enjoy what you are doing, and you will have regrets that will lead to unhappiness. Life is too short.

What's so important to me and to Joe is to show our daughter that you can do anything in life as long as you are able to move past roadblocks. Even when you might feel it's the end of the road, there's another green light ahead. It's okay to fall and get back up because you'll learn from those experiences.

We live in a town with many wealthy families and athletes, but everyone has a story about their struggle to get here. So, that's my wish: understand your dad's hustle. We worked *hard* to be where we are, and it was the struggles and the grind to get here that made our story what it is.

Joe never gave up. At one time in his life, Joe was at a very low point. He basically got rid of everything and started over. He was out of the mortgage company; he'd sold the salon...he started from scratch in his forties. To have that drive is wild because some people would just curl up in a hot corner and be like, "Oh, poor me, poor me." And he didn't. That drive was always there.

—Carla Tedeschi

One of the biggest surprises of being successful is how others view you. Most people view success from a monetary standpoint. This seems to define you to others. As I said in the beginning, financial wealth should not always be the definition of success. Achieving your personal goals is the true definition of success. Whether others accept that or not, you can be fulfilled and thus successful within yourself. Don't let success define you—*you* define you.

After my grandfather's death, my dad told me stories about him—what a great person he was, what a kind man he was, what a well-respected community member he was. The first Joe Tedeschi (Dad was "Junior") truly was the pillar of society. I knew he meant so much to so many people, including my father. After his death, I remember seeing Dad sitting in his chair in his bedroom the night he visited my grandmother. It was dark in the room, and I asked him, "What's wrong, Dad?" He summarized my grandfather and said things that truly resonated with me and words that I try to live by: "You will never find anyone who could say anything negative about your grandfather. To live your life like that is truly the sign of a great man." To this day, I will never forget those heartfelt words.

And now it's my time to create my gift for my family. I want Audrey to remember me as a good dad. I have talked a lot about different ways to define success throughout this book and how my grit and hard work has helped me put myself and my family in a good financial position. But the real thing that matters is that money helps create incredible memories, which will last forever. That is what I want my legacy to be about.

Acknowledgements

My appreciation to Tanya and Jeremy for their professional guidance throughout the acquisition process. Your expertise and support were invaluable, and I am indebted to you both. A special thank you to Tanya for your continued support even today; it means the world to me.

To Jeff and Christian, thank you for your professional guidance throughout the sale, making the process smooth and successful. I am truly grateful for your strategic guidance and insight.

Thank you Ed for believing in me and seeing my potential before anyone else.

My most heartfelt and special thanks to my friend Jimmy for providing me the opportunity to showcase my talents both in the workplace and as an individual. Together, we complemented each other like no other partners that I know could have, and we continue to find success with our dynamic duo strengths. I feel truly blessed to have you as my dearest and best friend. I love you, brother.

Mom and Dad, thank you for being my pillars of support. You were always there for me at so many times in my life and in so many ways that I can never come close to repaying you other than continuing to make you proud. Dad, I know you can't read this, but thank you for all you've done for me. You guided me, taught me, and inspired me like no one else. I aim to be like you and be that same type of dad to Audrey.

To my wife Carla, you are my best friend and the real reason I am who I am today. Your belief in me, even when I doubted myself, is the reason for my strength. You saw my potential when no one else did and made me believe in myself again. Your unwavering love that you had for me during my darkest days was what continued to push me to fight. I am truly grateful for all of you and admire how great of a mother you are to Audrey. I love you forever.

About The Author

Joe Tedeschi was born and raised in a small town in Rhode Island, the oldest of four children in a typical middle-class, Italian-American family. After attending the University of Southern California on an academic scholarship, he started, bought, and ran several businesses, including a soft frozen lemonade business, a bustling daytime coffee shop, a home improvement contracting network, a busy mortgage broker-age company, a one-of-its-kind online software company, and an upscale salon and spa, where he met his wife-to-be Carla in 2007.

In 2010, Joe joined his longtime friend Jimmy DeSisto to help grow his third-generation family pizza dough business, Venice Bakery, as they innovated and developed the new gluten-free era in consumer demand. As President of the company, Joe oversaw operations and specialized in

Brand Development, Market Analysis, Strategic Planning, and Business Negotiating. As part of his leadership, Venice Bakery went from generating about five million dollars annually to a nine-figure valuation at its sale to Rich Products in 2017. It was the largest acquisition in Rich Products' history at that time.

Today, Joe lives in Manhattan Beach, California, with his wife and beloved daughter, Audrey. He enjoys traveling, pursuing health and fitness, and spending time with his family.

www.ingramcontent.com/pod-product-compliance
Lightning Source LLC
Chambersburg PA
CBHW061141120626
46546CB00005B/1888